T0368436

The Ring Secret

Written by   Lady Canaday

Illustrated by   Dwain Esper

AuthorHouse™
1663 Liberty Drive
Bloomington, IN 47403
www.authorhouse.com
Phone: 1 (800) 839-8640

Published by AuthorHouse 04/16/2019

ISBN: 978-1-5049-5448-8 (sc)
ISBN: 978-1-5049-5450-1 (hc)
ISBN: 978-1-5049-5449-5 (e)

Library of Congress Control Number: 2015916385

Print information available on the last page.

authorHOUSE®

Dedication

This is dedicated to my departed dad and devoted mom, Marvin and Dorothy H., Jim and Mary S., every relative and friend who passed along the way, fifth graders, basketball fans, and all the celebrities who make a cameo appearance.

Acknowledgment

Special thanks to Marion H., my fifth-grade education consultant, for always being there to answer questions.

Inspiration

Transitioning from writing short stories to writing my first short novel happened as a result of wanting to challenge myself. The inspiration for this timely book came from our current state of the world.

Recommendation

This novella should be co-read with one or both parents at the preteen's pace. When you see a musical reference, pause the story, and listen to the song on the Internet to maximize your literary experience.

Contents

Chapter One

First Quarter

Opening

Today is Thursday, September 3, 2009, the first day of school due to a monthlong renovation delay. After the bell rings, teacher says: "Good morning, fifth graders. I'm Dr. Dorothy O'Brien. Welcome back to Arthur T. Wilson Elementary School."

After roll call, teacher states: "I'm a Nigerian-American wife of an Irish-American professional basketball player. My husband is Marvin 'Irish Marvel' O'Brien."

Shakobe says: "OMG! We're being punk'd. No way!" Dr. O'Brien tells: "Yes way! Marvin isn't a stuffed animal, my platonic plus-one, the object of my infatuation, a phantom, an imaginary guy, a hired fake boyfriend, my common-law spouse, or some print model pasted on my vision board. Our marriage certificate proves he's my bona-fide husband."

Lynn inquires: "When you were husband hunting, was a basketballer on your husband wish list?" Dr. O'Brien responds: "I wasn't a huntress looking for a love. Marrying a b-baller wasn't my endgame. No occupational preference on my HWL."

Valerie asks: "Were you a mail-order bride or runaway bride?" Dr. O'Brien says: "Never a mail-order bride. Shortly after the movie release of *Runaway Bride,* I was a *runway* bride at a benefit for underprivileged kids hosted by Julia Roberts."

Rebecca inquires: "Were you an encore bride like my mean, husband-stealing stepmomster?" Dr. O'Brien responds: "No remarriage here. We're each other's numero uno."

Sheet Cake asks: "Are you a midwife, too?" Dr. O'Brien answers: "Nope. Midwife means *with woman.* A midwife may be a woman or man medically trained to help with childbirth."

Tiny inquires: "Are you sure your fella isn't Creole, a Black albino, or half a brotha like that cutie-patootie hoopster from Minnesota?" Dr. O'Brien responds: "I've seen his Irish genealogy on a five-generation photo family tree. I'm convinced a secret branch doesn't exist and confident that he's not a biracial beige brotha or lacking pigmentation. Nor is he 100 percent wheat bread passing as white bread."

Charlotte says: "I don't think you're secretly White and wearing special-effect makeup or body paint, tanned, or popping melanin tablets. Could it be you're half a sista like *B.A.P.S* girl, Halle Barry?" Dr. O'Brien states, "I'm a full sista."

Dreadhead says: "Black professional athletes have pursued Beckies for eons, but a Barney pro basketballer down with brown *and* put a vow on it is unheard-of. Are you two in *The Guinness Book of World Records?*" Dr. O'Brien laughs and answers: "Uh-uh. According to my intel, we're possibly the first, but not the only."

Gracie says: "My mom has a work husband and my dad has a work wife. Is your work husband that El DeBarge look-alike teacher from Mumbai?" Dr. O'Brien responds: "No office spouse, but we both have a work family. Speaking of my esteemed colleague, Mr. Patel, he won our faculty/staff talent show in 2005. Whenever El is in town, he visits Mr. Patel's class. They wear matching outfits and perform Motown songs."

Ponytail says: "I once saw the honorary brotha and his entourage chilling with Paul Walker and Vin Diesel at an Indy 500. He's a global brand with bookoo endorsements like David Beckham. Are y'all Bill Gatin' in million-dollar rooms at your sprawling family compound, piece-of-the-pie penthouse, majestic villa, over-the-top estate, posh château, or on a mega yacht we can see on *MTV Cribs, The Fabulous Life Of...,* or *How'd You Get So Rich?*" Dr. O'Brien replies: "No, but years ago, I dreamt we were interviewed on Billionaires Beach by Robin Leach from *Lifestyles of the Rich and Famous*. We chatted about our champagne wishes and caviar dreams as the Eurythmics' 'Sweet Dreams' played."

Dr. O'Brien clears her throat and says: "Home court isn't a 90,000-square-foot mansion with a helipad and acreage for an amusement park. We aren't living large with a chef, maid staff, butler, chauffeur, topiary gardeners, and pool boy. Nor do we have personal assistants and wardrobe stylists. We're just suburbanites living the American Dream in a modest two-story abode. Our guard-gated community is near a picturesque country club. My humble husband doesn't want to be part of the 60 percent of professional basketball players who're broke within five years after retirement. Having a nest egg helps avoid bankruptcy, homelessness, depression, and suicide. Irish Marvel has to wait almost two decades to collect his full pension at 50."

Yingjie asks: "Does your Irishman have a supercool mantuary and tricked-out whips?" Dr. O'Brien answers: "Mantuary, yes. Tricked-out whips, not anymore. Irish Marvel and I found out the hard way those cars attract the wrong attention from Haterade drinkers. In 2003, we were traveling home from the ESPY Awards in our tricked-out Lambo. The two of us were riding low with Art Laboe, listening to Phil Collins' 'In the Air Tonight.' Shortly after the drum solo, we were carjacked at gunpoint by two burly women wearing masks." After hearing the couple's harrowing ordeal, class gasps.

Stevie inquires: "How'd your ballplayer husband get his nickname and where'd he go to college?" Dr. O'Brien says: "Marvin O'Brien was dubbed 'Irish Marvel' in 1997 after his hilarious Super Bowl commercial for a popular shaving cream company that capitalized on his Irishness. My husband along with Barry Bonds, Oscar De La Hoya, Wayne Gretzky, Andre Agassi, Walter Payton, and Rip Taylor spoofed *The $1.98 Beauty Show*. Marvin was a student-athlete in high school and graduated as salutatorian. He was a prep-to-pro player who was the top draft pick in June 1996. Marvin missed all of the hullabaloo surrounding March Madness. He didn't get to be a frat boy or a college Cinderella jock on a Cinderella team. Marvin wasn't a one-and-done collegiate player like most draftees since 2006."

Shakobe asks: "Why do you have three letters and two dots after your last name on the whiteboard?" Dr. O'Brien informs: "Ed.D. stands for Doctor of Education. The punctuation marks around the letters in my title are periods. A doctorate in America is a terminal degree, meaning the highest degree a person can get from a university. I graduated with a *research* doctorate from Harvard University, an Ivy League school. Doctors who practice medicine have a *professional* doctorate, medical license, and prescription pad."

Charlotte comments: "That totally kills my dingbat socialite/trophy wife theory." Ivy Leaguer smiles and responds: "I'm a *capable* wife who occasionally attends social events to take a breather from working inside and outside the home. Besides, my husband says that a *trophy* belongs in a display case."

Gracie says: "You must be one smart cookie. They don't let anybody just waltz into that institution of higher learning. I thought maybe you're an honorary doc like Dr. Maya Angelou. Glad you're not a quack, charlatan, or snake oil saleswoman. Did you have a white coat ceremony for your graduation?" Smart Cookie answers: "No. First-year medical students in med school receive short white laboratory coats at a formal robing ceremony to welcome them. Today's homework is to define the noun A-U-T-O-D-I-D-A-C-T, research the meaning of an Ivy League school, and list the other prestigious seven. Your assignment is due tomorrow. Doctor's orders."

Mary Starlett tells: "My great-aunt was like you. She had reverse jungle fever, but no swirl babies. Her ex-Black Panther folks back in Sag Harbor, New York, didn't believe in mixing and melting the Black race. So, to get their approval for marriage, she had to bring home a guy who could share her comb. Second time around, her folks were already six feet under and was free to try something new. Aunt Cat met her rainbeau, Uncle Wes, in church. She used to always tell me and my sisters that finding a good man is like finding a needle in a haystack."

Dr. O'Brien adjusts the thermostat. Pupils talk and wonder how the couple met. Teacher hears them and says: "He wasn't my secret admirer or congregant interested in me. We didn't meet winking and flirting at a Build-A-Bear Workshop, sharing a love seat, at Chuck E. Cheese's, dueling on *Family Feud*, in line at Starbucks, ziplining, playing musical chairs at a bat mitzvah, renting a bounce house, at a charity masquerade ball, skiing in Aspen, getting green slimed at the Kids' Choice Awards, on a blind date, or at a roach coach. Nor did it happen playing Spin the Bottle, in an elevator, at the raunchy pole dancing place, doing a Semester at Sea program, at a memorial service, taking the Twizzler challenge, kayaking, at a spelling bee, spelunking, at a divorce party, bar-hopping, at a toga party, twerking at a Sadie Hawkins dance, playing Twister, in traffic school, grabbing matching bookends at a garage sale, attending a White House dinner, treating a hickey, crowd-surfing, at a road game on Black Friday, dodging gluten-free fruitcake at an ugly Christmas sweater party, or grappling for the last eggnog at a Kwanzaa potluck. I'm game for other guesses."

Tiny guesses: "You kept your mystery guy as your little secret because you were the only lady jockey at the Kentucky Derby and he owned your racehorse." Dr. O'Brien replies: "A Black female hasn't rocked the K.D. as a jockey, trainer, or owner. However, Black male jockeys were the first U.S. sports superstars."

Ponytail guesses: "Your reformed bad boy was popping bottles in a club's VIP section with his catcalling homies while searching for his latest chase-and-conquest chick. Right after his hawk-eyed wingman spotted you among the throng on ladies' night, Irish Marvel told you a filthy pick-up line you can't repeat to kids, he got too handsy, and you kneed his nuggets." Dr. O'Brien responds: "Behaving like a boorish, pie-eyed skirt-chaser isn't his style."

Ray Ray guesses: "You were already seeing someone – not a techie buppie or some scruffy country bumpkin or a suave Casanova – just an average Joe. Y'all weren't exclusive or serious. Still, you felt really guilty for falling head over heels in love when the free agent hit on you after selling him fudge at a school bake sale." Dr. O'Brien says, "Nope."

Dr. O'Brien achoos twice, and then states: "It's a bird, it's a plane, it's Superboy." Class clown guesses: "A nice fishwife knew you had a thing for him. So, she introduced you to the great catch." Teacher says: "He wasn't the catch of the day at a you-buy-we-fry fish market."

Lynn guesses: "Being one of the guys and a sister figure weren't enough anymore. So, you snooped around and found out the senior bachelor you liked only thought of you as a daughter figure. Week later, your birthday wish for a younger bachelor came true when the holder of the key to your heart swept you off your feet at a lock and key singles mixer." Dr. O'Brien states: "No."

Dreadhead guesses: "Rather than play hard-to-get or wait for *him* to make a move on you, a voice in your head told *you* to make the first move. So, after you had some liquid courage, you snatched him up by giving him the come-hither finger on St. Paddy's Day at an Irish pub during happy hour." Dr. O'Brien responds: "Nope. Nor did we meet by pinching for not wearing green that holiday."

Betty guesses: "You had a really bad breakup, lost your mojo, was tired of being a third or fifth wheel, and refused to buy a boyfriend pillow or man-share. So, during a girls' night out, your pushy, but well-meaning bestie set up y'all on a dare. He wasn't perfect on paper or your type. Yet, somehow Mr. Not Quite grew on you and eventually you were bitten by the love bug." Dr. O'Brien says, "Airrrrrrr ball."

Monobrow overhears the discussion, pops his head through the door, and guesses: "Your *fate mate* snagged you at an O'Bryan concert on hump day. The dude blew you a kiss, you caught it, and blew one back. Intermission came, y'all talked, had instant chemistry, he got the digits, and your lovelite been turned on ever since." Dr. O'Brien hums Digital Underground's "Kiss You Back" and replies: "Entertaining, but incorrect. Monobrow, you better get to class. You don't want demerits or detention on day one."

Dr. O'Brien shuts the classroom door as Gracie guesses: "On a scavenger hunt with your nieces and nephews, you picked up a dandelion, made a wish, and blew the puffball. Suddenly, the man of your dreams appeared." Teacher responds: "No. Nor did we meet at some wishing well, on Blueberry Hill, or in Rome at the famous Trevi Fountain."

Rebecca guesses: "Not looking forward to another manic Monday, you called in sick to play hooky from work for a pampering spa day and some retail therapy. Still in your jammies, you were love-struck at your doorstep by a sharp-dressed Jehovah's Witness who was simply irresistible and so into you that you didn't care what he had to say about the Bible or *The Watchtower* and *Awake!* magazines." Moments later, Dr. O'Brien has a ZZ Top *Pop UP Video* flashback and comments: "A dashing, well-versed gent with that kinda hypnotic swag hasn't knocked on my front door. It wasn't lust, love, or married at first sight."

B-Raid guesses: "Love blossomed after his pastor, Tupac, Biggie, Michael Jordan, or Patti Stanger, the millionaire matchmaker, hooked y'all up." Dr. O'Brien answers: "We weren't fixed up through a mutual friend, family member, matchmaker, marriage broker, or miracle worker."

Rudy guesses: "His skinny, superficial, no-good, undeserving, exotic-looking GF bailed on *him* behind some bull *she* started. Next day, your dreamlover was sprucing up his bachelor pad for all-star weekend when you were suddenly a damsel in distress who flopped into his strong arms at Home Depot." Dr. O'Brien replies: "Dreamlover didn't rescue me. Time allows for one more guess."

Charlotte guesses: "You heard that golden oldie 'Want Ads,' joined Match.com, and then gave romance a chance when he asked you out." Dr. O'Brien responds: "Neither I nor a secret someone signed me up for digital love. After I got married, I heard positive things about BlackPeopleMeet.com, eHarmony.com, and some mobile dating apps. The thought of shopping myself on the Internet, having feelings for someone, and possibly getting catfished *still* gives me the heebie-jeebies. There was no vetting or intervening on our behalves. We met at a city library on Friday, February 19, 1999. Irish Marvel and I clicked on all cylinders and started a whirlwind courtship."

Betty asks: "Did his meddlesome folks go to anger management class because he listened to his heart and chose a brownie bride who ties her hair up at bedtime instead of a snow bride who wakes up with bed-head hair?" Dr. O'Brien informs: "They didn't meddle. Both are crazy about moi, their daughter-in-law. I didn't have to win them over since I wasn't ghetto, an experiment, challenge, inheritance necessity, part of some get-married-by-a-certain-date pact, novelty, spring fling, bait in a bet, runner-up, wild card, his teammate's mom, or some weave-wearing, fake-lady-parts, flavor-of-the-month party girl, or worst of all, somebody who gives love a bad name. His folks knew that I didn't pursue him, rush him, pressure him, seduce him, or trap him. They were in seventh heaven their chick-magnet son was off the market and found a good woman to marry into the family."

Kathy Rose says: "Obviously, you didn't find your ideal *Black* man. Did your interfering parents have a hissy fit because you followed your heart and chose a snowman rather than a gingerbread man?" Dr. O'Brien says: "Obviously, he didn't find his ideal *White* woman. My parents were on cloud nine knowing my pursuer wasn't a bird dog, slobbish man-child, or an Irish toad, but rather a well-brought-up man with integrity who'd treat me like a lady. They knew I wasn't a sellout, Oreo, money-hungry, desperate, craving validation, ego-tripping, project manager looking for a new project, seeking fame and a jet-set lifestyle, rebelling against them, or settling for Mr. Good Enough out of fear of being alone forever. My parents wanted to marry off their daughter who's an eight-time bouquet-catching champ. A prospective mate was a godsend. It meant the Silent Generation (born 1928-1945) empty nesters were one step closer to getting lineal grandkids or adoptive grandkids and didn't have to fill the void with grandcats and granddogs. Interfering could've derailed hope for their third act of life. Finally, extended family, friends, and prying pesterers could cease asking me 'why're you still minus a man,' stop hoping and praying I'm next, quit sympathetically telling me 'your time will come' year after year, cease calling me 'leftover lady,' 'poor thing,' and 'old maid,' stop assuming my life is lacking meaning no matter what I accomplish, and quit thinking I'm headed to the Lonely Old Ladies Cat and Knit Club. Best of all, people could stop judging my parents for my being above 30 without a chap and children, and cease believing I'd be Miss Neveruary lying in a mortuary before being asked to marry."

Superboy asks: "When you and Hungry Eyes first got boo'd up, didya hafta sign a keep-your-mouth-shut, celebrity thingy?" Dr. O'Brien responds: "No. I'd never sign a nondisclosure agreement a.k.a. confidentiality agreement to be with anyone."

Shakobe inquires: "Before mailing save-the-date cards, invitations, and choosing a china pattern for your wedding registry, did you and the lucky guy sign a whatchamacallit?" Lucky Girl answers: "We didn't have to jump through hoops for each other and quote Kanye West by hollering, 'We want prenup!' A prenup is short for prenuptial agreement. We didn't ink a *pre*nuptial agreement to protect money and property *before* our nuptials nor did we put our John Hancock on a *post*nuptial agreement to protect money and property *after* our nuptials."

Dr. O'Brien refills a glue container and explains: "The reasons were the following: (1) we didn't get married on a whim, (2) we knew marriage is a sacred privilege with God as the center strand of an invisible threefold cord, (3) we didn't have a rocky Hollywood marriage headed directly to splitsville with an annulment, and (4) God hates a divorce decree for reasons other than cheating. A safety net for first-timers isn't necessary if the foundation is built on trust and loyal love."

Ray Ray asks: "Does that mean y'all will live happily ever after like make-believe couples in those Disney once-upon-a-time fairy tales?" Dr. O'Brien replies: "No. Our king-and-queen story will try to find happily-ever-after as real life happens."

Gracie inquires: "Before saying 'yes' to the dress and taking the walk in white, did you and him get engaged, start a family, and then test-drive marriage by shacking up like La La and Carmelo?" Dr. O'Brien states: "N-to-the-O! We did things in the right order and here's why: Since 1994, 72 percent of Black kids are born to single moms. We refused to contribute to that disgraceful statistic! Shacking up in a love nest by living together on a full-time basis or having a stayover relationship by living together on a part-time basis is backwards and most likely a stall tactic. It's usually the breadwinner's way to merge onto the freeway of love. Cautionary tale: Significant others like Brangelina who live together beforehand, may never hear wedding bells chime. Step skippers often live in limbo, take longer to get married, and have a higher rate of divorce. Cohabitation a.k.a. shacking up and the trendy stayover key-and-a-drawer relationship are sugarcoated expressions for living in sin. Living together for however many days is for insecure marriage pretenders who wanna play house like preschoolers."

Tiny asks: "Didja use your Black girl magic to cast a love spell at your place by wearing a little black dress and setting the mood for an intimate dinner with soft music, candlelight, and making Engagement Chicken to get your BF to propose, or were you a frantic romantic who did a 180 by flying to Ireland for Leap Day to ask your big baller boo to marry you?" Dr. O'Brien answers: "Reeling him in by creating the perfect ambiance for Operation Poultry Proposal Plan wasn't some drawn up play on my clipboard. I may be a rom-com fanatic, but I wouldn't dream of denying my beau the honor of proposing on that quadrennial day (February 29) or any other."

Shakobe asks: "Did your *love* daddy hafta ask your *real* daddy for your hand in marriage?" Dr. O'Brien responds: "Since I was going to be a late bloomer bride, Irish Marvel didn't need my old man's permission or blessing. Love Daddy knew my real daddy wouldn't rudely spurn his request. Being a gentleman, he wanted to ask his future father-in-law *and* future mother-in-law. That impressive game plan scored their future son-in-law buckets of brownie points."

Dr. O'Brien thumbs a workbook and tells: "Last year, Cecil and L.M. wanted to know if my guy ever gave me false proposal hope with Tiffany diamond earrings or a rock in a Cartier ring box. I told them he wouldn't sink my heart like that."

Lynn says: "Sounds like he was a winner playing for keeps and not a lying dog stringing you along or a foot-dragger scared to take the logical next step. Clearly, he was emotionally available, ready to settle down, and wanted to forsake all others. So, how'd Irish Marvel propose?" Dr. O'Brien says: "After four months of wooing me, he professed his undying love. On Saturday, June 19, 1999, my suitor recited romantic poetry, knelt down on his left knee, and asked me the customary WYMM-question under a Rose Moon at a scenic botanical garden. He proposed there because the first wedded couple, Adam and Eve, who were married by God, began their life together in the Garden of Eden. He declared his honorable intentions with a placeholder, heart-shaped e-ring. It was a strawberry-flavored Valentine Ring Pop."

Students ask, "Did you eat it?" Dr. O'Brien replies: "It's preserved with a spray that keeps creepy-crawlies away. If we lived in colonial times, I would've received a thimble. After the wedding, the top would've been cut off and the thimble would be worn as my w-ring. Back to the proposal, the lighted ring box played the music to 'Marriage-God's Arrangement.' Next afternoon, Irish Marvel drove me, the bride-elect, to his jeweler. My fiancé confirmed to the world that our engagement was official with a fog-tested, heart-shaped diamond solitaire. FYI: A betrothal a.k.a. engagement without a set wedding date within one year is a red flag one or both aren't ready to be joined in holy matrimony."

Yingjie inquires: "Didja get your knight in shining armor a man-gagement ring?" Dr. O'Brien responds: "They weren't popular back then. If I were engaged today, I'd requite my love by buying him one so his ringless left hand wouldn't scream, 'I'm Mr. Available!' "

Shakobe is overheard asking Ray Ray: "How do gay couples pop the question? Who flips the coin to pick the last name?" Dr. O'Brien tells: "My gay Avon lady, Mary Kay, told me that there's no PTQ rule for gay couples. She said that with or without a ring, one partner may ask first, take turns asking, or both may look at each other and say, 'Let's get married!' According to Mary Kay, the last name is whatever a couple choose."

Ponytail says: "We know you didn't blackout, hightail it, or barf all over him *and* the ring during an ambush proposal like my mom's double cousin. I guess nobody told her that it's bad luck to see the ring before the moment of truth. For fun, did you make your jolly good fellow sweat before you answered the four-word question?" Dr. O'Brien responds: "First, I saw Alex Trebek standing at his podium. Next, the 30-second tick-tock tune for Final Jeopardy! played in my head for a split second, and then I plighted my troth to him with a resounding 'yes.' After agreeing to be his fiancée, Larry Graham stepped out of a lavender hydrangea bush and crooned 'When We Get Married.' " Dolf asks: "Did Larry Graham also croon 'One in a Million You'?" Teacher answers, "No."

Floppy asks: "Is courting what mallrats do at a food court or something done on a b-ball court, with a court jester, in a courtyard, or inside a courthouse courtroom with Judge Jude?" Dr. O'Brien tells: "Courting is something a man and woman do off the court."

Sheet Cake inquires: "Isn't having a gentleman caller, going steady, handwriting love letters back and forth, and courting what old fogies call *dating?*" Dr. O'Brien explains: "Today's what's-love-got-to-do-with-it dating attitude is going out with many people without a purpose. It's done repeatedly, is never-ending, and nothing is off-limits. Serial daters who marry are often one-day planners and have no idea what their lives will be like after the wedding. Courtship is a different playbook. It isn't just about Mr. Chivalry arriving with flowers and chocolate to take a woman out for dinner and a movie. It's for life planners who are ready to consider marriage and only done with someone you'd consider marrying. Courtshippers do romantic activities. Equally important, they have confidential talks about their feelings, dreams, fears, goals, and expectations of life after all the hoopla surrounding the big day. Courtship should only occur once. However, it may happen more than once if one of them perishes prior to marriage, a couple decide to remain in the friend zone, or if somebody's spouse joins the cemetery or cremation club, making a wife a *widow* or a husband a *widower.*"

B-Raid asks: "How old do you gotta be to start a courtship?" Dr. O'Brien responds: "Ideally, in your twenties or any decade thereafter." Next, she whistles the melody to Sam Cooke's "Wonderful World." Afterward, teacher tells: "When my truelove and I were tweens, our parents warned us about the hazards of toying with romance in elementary school, middle school/JHS, and high school. They were right about dating before high school graduation being a time-consuming distraction to keep youngsters away from spiritual growth, family, school, and friends."

Rebecca inquires: "Are you talking about some crush, puppy love, or Romeo and Juliet?" Dr. O'Brien hums Janet Jackson's "Young Love," and then says: "Sussudio! All the above. Those love-is-in-the-air feelings are real, natural, and a self-esteem booster. However, it's best not to act on them until you're a mature adult."

Dr. O'Brien answers the classroom phone. When the call ends, teacher continues: "Our folks also cautioned us about the dangers of casually dating as adults. Women who casually date usually wind up kissing gobs of figurative frogs to weed out Prince *Harming* in their quest for Prince *Charming*. FYI: Kissing literal frogs is hazardous because amphibians are salmonella carriers. One advantage of marriage is that you can go on romantic *mate dates* forever."

Stevie asks, "How long is a courtship?" Dr. O'Brien says: "The length should be discussed in advance. One year or less is ideal to avoid frustration and temptation."

Kathy Rose inquires: "So, if somebody acts up during a courtship, is the guilty person court-martialed?" Dr. O'Brien explains: "Civilians don't go to military court. Court-martial is only for military crimes."

Fran asks: "Why do grown-ups say that relationships are complicated?" Dr. O'Brien replies: "Sweetie, complicated is a code word/excuse for adults when they don't want to talk about an uncomfortable relationship. This usually happens when they hit a relationship roadblock or there's a web of wrongdoing surrounding it."

Lynn inquires: "Were you one of those spendaholic June brides with a no-limit black card?" Dr. O'Brien says: "No way, José! Our financial planners, Suze Orman and Clark Howard, helped us stay within our budget. J.Lo, our wedding planner, saved this bridechilla from becoming a bridezilla."

Rebecca asks: "When your turn *finally* came to become one with someone, didja get dolled up in a Vera Wang wedding gown and your proud pa gave you away after marching to 'Here Comes the Bride' or did you and the apple of your eye do the envelope thing?" Dr. O'Brien says: "I doubt that fashion designer makes ethnic wedding attire. I wore an African wedding dress to honor my Nigerian culture. Irish Marvel wore a kilt to honor his Irish culture. We didn't *elope*. My betrothed and I didn't have a civil ceremony or go with a tropical backdrop. We had a destination wedding at a ranch fit for a king. 'Here Comes the Bride' originates from the 1850 German opera called *Lohengrin*. Richard Wagner's dramatic music is played with lyrics performed by women in the wedding party *after* a couple's wedding. The groom, Lohengrin, abandons his bride, Elsa, on their wedding night causing the grief-stricken wife to drop dead."

Superboy states: "Speaking of kilts, is it true Irish and Scottish dudes don't wear underpants with their wooly man-skirts?" Class giggles and Dr. O'Brien answers: "I also wondered until I asked my husband. He told me that underwear *is* required for modesty sake for players and dancers participating in the Highland Games. Other than that, it's just preference." Superboy asks: "So, on your wedding day, did he go Captain Underpants-less?" Teacher chuckles and replies, "I'll never tell."

Dr. O'Brien sips white tea and starts the wedding story: "We tied the knot the morning of Sunday, September 19, 1999, at Michael Jackson's Neverland Ranch. Weather-wise, we chose the ninth month because it falls in the Goldilocks Zone. Boy George did my makeup. You'll never guess in a million years who did my hair." Kids guess, "Vidal Sassoon," "Elgin Charles," "José Eber," "Paul Mitchell," "Real from *Real Chance of Love*." Teacher responds, "George Clinton." Students ask, "The 'Atomic Dog' singer?" Dr. O'Brien answers: "Yep. Long before the Godfather of Funk became the bandleader of Parliament-Funkadelic, he worked at a barber salon. Sidebar: Spiritual unions for a man and woman aren't the same as getting married. Commitment ceremonies for two men or two women also aren't the same as getting married. Those married-in-our-hearts celebrations don't count law-wise because a marriage license isn't required."

Dr. O'Brien sharpens a #2 pencil and states: "The procession went well. Etta James sang 'Sunday Kind of Love.' We had seven bridesmaids, seven groomsmen. There was no maid of honor or best man. Jill, my cuz's poodle, was the hound of honor. Bugsy, his pug, was the best dog. Standing alongside the floral arch with us were Mr. Haddadi, our Middle Eastern minister, Corinne, our Asian ring bearer, and Rogelio, our Latino flower boy."

Dr. O'Brien finishes her white tea and says: "The cutest ceremony moment happened right after our minister stated: 'The bride's and the groom's matching diamond bands are each 2,500 carats.' Corinne pointed at the minister and yelled: 'Liar, liar, pants on fire! Carrots are orange veggies Bugs Bunny eats.' After everybody stopped laughing, Corinne's mom, Nadine, walked up to Corinne and whispered: 'The carats mean the *weight* of the jewels on their wedding bands.' After the bridegroom lifted my veil and our marriage vows were sealed with an amorous kiss, we jumped over an ornate broom. Jumping the broom is an African tradition that's popular at African-American weddings. My ancestors weren't permitted to legally marry. So, slaves honored their unions by jumping the broom. We did it to symbolize our yoke of marriage as sweeping away singlehood and a leap into a new adventure. During the recession, a gorgeous ginger-haired Irishwoman wearing Irish garb named Shamrock Sheelagh played Irish music with uilleann pipes. It was important to us to incorporate something for the ceremony from both our heritages."

Teacher refills her stapler and begins the reception story: "At the reception, we had a Sunday brunch. MJ and Siedah Garrett sang 'I Just Can't Stop Loving You.' We substituted the ho-hum traditional bridal waltz for a choreographed first dance with the King of Pop to 'Black or White.' " Gracie replies: "Did the video go viral on YouTube?" Teacher says: "Nope, but it could've generated enough hits to be one of the top ten all-time first dance videos."

Dr. O'Brien restocks construction paper and tells: "A funny reception moment was during the bouquet toss while Cyndi Lauper sang 'Girls Just Want to Have Fun.' Midway through Cyndi's performance, Bubbles, MJ's chimpanzee, swooped down a banana tree wearing a turquoise tuxedo. Bubbles caught my toss bouquet with his teeth and scratched his head afterward. Another amusing moment happened during the garter toss. My toss garter landed on Louie the Llama's left ear as Cameo's 'Single Life' played. Everybody laughed and danced to 'Louie Louie' by The Kingsmen. My favorite reception moment happened when The O'Jays performed 'Love Train' in front of the train station. A conga line was formed. When the lyrics said England, Russia, China, Africa, Egypt, Israel, The O'Jays paused while school-age kids dressed from each nation performed a cultural dance. After that, everyone boarded *Katherine*, Michael's choo-choo train. Later, before cutting the wedding cake, Robert Palmer rocked the house when he performed 'Addicted to Love.' Etta James ended the reception singing 'At Last.' "

Yingjie says: "Your wee-day must've been off the chandelier! Can we see some wedding pictures on your website or Spacebook page?" Dr. O'Brien answers: "Neither of us has a *Myspace* page or *Facebook* page. Our storybook wedding was positively one of the best days of our lives. Mi amor and I were deliriously happy. We considered releasing some photos to *Essence* and *People* but decided to remember the time by keeping recorded memories as private keepsakes."

Betty inquires: "Are you mad at the *milk doc* who left Prince, Paris, and Blanket without a dad?" Dr. O'Brien picks up an autographed picture of Captain EO from her desk, kisses the sunflower frame, and weepingly responds: "Whenever MJ's family, friends, and fans reminisce about him, our hearts are equally divided with happiness and sadness because he's gone too soon. Dr. Murray and MJ is a tragic friendship story that's a school-of-life lesson for everyone. Sometimes, saying 'no' is the hardest and best way to help a friend."

Fran asks, "Where'd you and your unicorn go on your honeymoon?" Dr. O'Brien remembers her two-week unpaid leave and answers: "We spent five days at a castle in the Emerald Isle and five days at a palace in the Dark Continent."

Kathy Rose inquires: "What does honey hafta do with the moon?" Dr. O'Brien explains: "*Honey* part implies that marital love is sweet like honey in the beginning. *Moon* part implies that marital love will wane like the moon, meaning it'll be less sweet as time goes on."

Shakobe tells: "My pitiful 55-year-old unc boohooed like a baby and went on a solomoon. That's a honeymoon for one. He jetted to Bora Bora shortly after his 17-year-old child bride stood him up at the altar and ran off with the 64-year-old preacher. Man, that heartless hussy just dumped him like he was smelly garbage! My heartbroken uncle was so bummed; Dr. Phil was useless."

Charlotte asks: "Back in Ireland, did you two chug green beer and Irish whiskey, kiss the famous Blarney Stone upside-down, belt out 'My Wild Irish Rose,' or luck upon any Riverdancing leprechauns with a pot of gold at the end of a rainbow?" Dr. O'Brien says: "No. Those mischievous elves aren't real. That's Irish folklore you see on TV and at the theater." Class responds, "What's folklore?" Teacher explains: "They're local stories passed down by folks in a community or country."

Floppy states: "I've never seen Black people on the small screen or big screen with Irish storylines. Is it 'cause they're only at the U.S. Embassy?" Dr. O'Brien answers: "Blacks have been in Ireland since the mid-1500s. Ireland's capital and biggest city, Dublin, has the highest Black population."

Dreadhead says: "You're married. So, why're we calling you *Dr.* O'Brien instead of *Mrs.* O'Brien?" Teacher thinks about the album cover poster of Donna Summer's "She Works Hard for the Money" hanging on the wall in her lady lair and explains: "In the workforce, it's hard for a woman to drop her doctor title just because she's spoken for."

B-Raid proffers a splendiferous suggestion: "If you wear a *long* white coat like the children's doctor, it'll be easier for us to remember to call you *Dr.* O'Brien." Teacher replies, "Okay, like a pediatrician."

Gracie says: "My mom is the only girl, an attorney, and a feminist. After she told me what that F-word means, she said that modern professional women should always keep their birth name. So, when my mom married my dad, he had no choice, but to suck it up." Dr. O'Brien responds: "In America, it's tradition that a woman takes her husband's last name when she marries. Nowadays, some women hyphenate their last names by putting a hyphen between their maiden name and married name. Some progressive couples choose a different direction by creating a blended last name or the husband changes his last name to the wife's last name. For *me*, my decision was easy: *one* family – kids or no kids – means *one* last name."

Lynn states: "One night, I got my fright on by watching a scary movie where two people became one flesh. I was petrified like that Gloria Gaynor song for a month! How does a bride and groom become one flesh in real life?" Dr. O'Brien explains: "The expression *one flesh* comes from Scriptures in the Bible a.k.a. the Good Book at Genesis 2:24, Matthew 19:5-6, Mark 10:6-8, and Ephesians 5:28-31. It means a married couple operate together as a unit in *every* aspect of their lives."

Rebecca tells: "My Sunday school teacher said that the Bible is the best-selling book of all times. Mackenzie, my next-door neighbor, is an atheist. She doesn't believe in God, Scriptures, prayers, or guardian angels. Every summer, Mackenzie's parents send her to an atheist camp to be with other atheist kids. Although something tells me that she and her atheist amigos would call on God if a bear, Bigfoot, or the boogeyman comes after them."

Dr. O'Brien's ring glistens from the sunlight. Gracie states: "Dang! That's no gumball ring, Cracker Jack ring, or tacky hand-me-down mood ring. Your bling sparkles like diamonds in a cartoon. Is it a birthday present from Elizabeth Taylor, contest prize from Zsa Zsa Gabor, or something you got at a Marilyn Monroe auction?" Teacher answers: "It's not an heirloom or costume jewelry from HSN. The conversation piece is my authentic, one-of-a-kind wedding ring."

Valerie says: "Your whopper is *way* bigger than Wendy William's wedding ring. Rocketeers can see yours from outer space!" Dr. O'Brien replies: "Wendy is a friend in my head." Instantly, teacher daydreams she's having couch chat with Wendy while holding Shakeetha, Wendy's wig head.

Sheet Cake asks: "Do married people have to wear wedding rings?" Dr. O'Brien explains: "They aren't required for the M-word. Before World War II, which took place between 1939 and 1945, married men in the U.S. rarely wore them. American military men started the custom to remember their wives back home. Nowadays, most couples exchange rings during a double-ring ceremony as they're a visible symbol of pride and loyalty. They also signify stepping into the future together."

Ponytail inquires: "Why are wedding rings always worn on the left fourth finger?" Dr. O'Brien responds: "Before autopsy, the exam to find the cause of death, people believed the ring finger was the only one with a vein that ran directly to the heart. Today, doctors know that's a myth. In America, time-honored tradition dictates that they're worn on the *we* side as opposed to the *me* side."

Superboy says: "I was told that the Pope, priests, and habit-wearing penguin ladies from *Sister Act* can't get married." Dr. O'Brien explains: "The Pope, priests, and *nuns* take a vow of chastity and don't get married so they can devote their lives to the Catholic Church."

Mary Starlett tells: "I heard nuns wear wedding rings and claim they're married to Jesus." Dr. O'Brien clarifies: "Nuns view themselves as *spiritual* brides of Christ. All nuns don't wear them. Sometimes, a wedding band is worn to indicate which convent the nun performs her duties."

After recess, Dreadhead asks: "What's that square doodad over there with the flowers and tomato-red lips?" Dr. O'Brien says: "Bliss Kiss Chart. The silk flowers are called kissing balls. Flower girls may carry them at weddings. Kissing balls are sometimes used for decorations at home or parties. During my husband's visits, we always kiss to the instrumental version of 'Kiss' by Prince. While we're kissing, class counts aloud how long our kiss lasts. Once we are done with the love thang, I record the pertinent data on the chart. Subsequently, everybody enjoys one piece of Hershey's Bliss White Chocolate Meltaway and one piece of Hershey's Kisses. The candies symbolize our Black-and-White love. Last school day, we determine how many times we kissed as well as the shortest and longest kiss."

Dr. O'Brien shows a picture of blue roses and tells: "Whenever my husband visits, he always brings me a dozen blue roses. You're probably asking yourselves: 'How can roses be blue like Smurfs?' " Students nod "yes." Teacher explains: "Scientists called biotechnologists have grown them in laboratories since 2004. A florist can dye white roses to blue or any other color. White roses can be dyed at home using food coloring and H_2O. Leaves can also be dyed any color."

Betty inquires: "Did you get fed up, give up on finding your Nubian prince, and totally lose faith in Black love like all the man-bashing, scorned old biddies in my auntie Margie's book club?" Dr. O'Brien says, "Au contraire." Gracie responds: "Speaking of books, is it true women are supposed to act like a lady, but think like a man when it comes to matters of the heart?" Teacher recalls The Monotones' "The Book of Love" and answers: "Yes, if you ask Steve Harvey. Personally, I'd much rather get relationship pearls of wisdom from Herbert and Zelmyra Fisher. Their 85-year marriage makes them the oldest-living married couple."

Floppy asks: "Are you afraid your husband will call you the six-letter N-word or you'll call him the bird word?" Dr. O'Brien explains: "That's never been a concern. Those inflammatory words weren't in our vocabulary before we intermarried."

Rudy inquires: "Is it true that love is blind?" Dr. O'Brien recollects the 1965 movie, *A Patch of Blue*, and answers, "It can be."

Valerie says: "Some of my dad's buddies dipped in the snow a lot like O.J. Simpson. One of my mom's gal pals played in the snow many times like Whoopi Goldberg. I know God doesn't have voice mail set up. So, I'm wondering if you asked God by knee mail to send your checklist guy but forgot to request what color you wanted." Former blackchelorette tells: "There was no divine intervention oversight on my part. Nor did I dream up a 'Dear Future Husband' song or drop a line to Santa by snail mail. A snowmance was just how the cookie dough turned out. Marrying the most eligible blackchelor would have been picture-perfect for a Black excellence greeting card. Nonetheless, I was and still OK with the *right* stuff packaged in the *white* stuff."

Floppy inquires: "Were your Black girlfriends totally weirded out about you marrying the White Shadow?" Dr. O'Brien responds: "Some were at first, but they *totally* dug his Irish accent. Once they saw for themselves that I married an amazing man with great character, his skin color didn't matter."

Mary Starlett says: "My mommy is Black and light-skinned like hair-whipping Willow Smith. My daddy is Black and dark-skinned like you. Before boarding the love boat with your White dreamboat dude, did you ever once try light-and-dark Black love?" Dr. O'Brien tells: "Before sailing the *Irish* Sea, I sailed the *Black* Sea. My long-lost love from my early 20s had movie-star good looks with a medium brown complexion. Devondre and I reconnected in my late 30s and cruised the sea of love briefly. Our ship sank when he died of AIDS from a blood transfusion. Speaking of transfusion, can pregnant women donate blood?" Class responds, "Uh-huh." Teacher explains: "It's too risky for the mom and baby's health. The Bible states at Acts 15:29 to abstain from blood (human and animal) for good health. Screening donated blood for *every* illness under the sun is impossible. Thankfully, bloodless alternatives can be requested."

Three weeks later is Back-to-School Night. Walking the long hallway, Dr. O'Brien says "hello" to a foreign exchange student, an overachiever, an underachiever, Muslim room mom, fanhawk-wearing tutor nicknamed "Birdie-Birdie," a student named Larry O'Brien, gold star dad, a refugee, cafeteria worker, lay teacher at a parochial school, truant officer, school secretary, PTA members, crossing guard Butch, latchkey kid, school bus driver, Little League standout dubbed "Jackrabbit," DREAMer/immigration activist, school superintendent, and hoodie-sporting Trayvon who's downing a pack of Skittles. She also sees a problem child and silently prays for the troubled girl with a stank attitude.

Shortly thereafter, Dr. O'Brien runs into Allen, a spunky kid known around the playground as "A.I." Teacher says, "I heard you were in Turkey." A.I. responds: "Nah. The grapevine was wrong. My family and I are going to Istanbul *next* October." Teacher replies: "Sweetie, when you get there, send me a postcard."

Bobby McFerrin's "Don't Worry, Be Happy" plays while Dr. O'Brien welcomes parents as they enter her classroom. Next, she passes around a curriculum handout and introduces her towering husband. Teacher opens her presentation with a Phyllis Diller icebreaker joke. Afterward, she dazzles parents with a slideshow of activities, projects, field trips, and experiments planned for the school year.

Dr. O'Brien explains to the parents why she wears a long white coat in the classroom. Next, teacher surprises her pupils by giving them short white coats to wear in class. Each lab coat has the learner's name embroidered above the left chest pocket like hers. At the conclusion of the presentation, she posts her e-mail address on the whiteboard and asks if anyone has questions. Much to her surprise, nobody raises a *my child* question or any other.

After the presentation, middle-class families stay and chew the fat. During the remaining minutes of the hour-long event, teacher thanks everyone for coming and reassures them by playing Bob Marley's "Everything's Gonna Be Alright" as they exit.

Sheet Cake bumps into Dr. O'Brien later and relays: "Superboy's pop said that you're B-A-D and a helluva game-changer. Rebecca's Cruella-esque stepmother mentioned something about a hellcat, lucrative love, and said that the only reason you saw a future with moola man is because you're a greedy granny groupie who hit pay dirt. B-Raid's big mama said that you and your charismatic adonis really flipped the script. Dreadhead's stay-at-home mom said that you're one of those long-in-the-tooth GCBs who had a midlife crisis. Gracie's auntie said that Frosty is fwine. Rudy's hairy papi said that you're an over-the-hill, hot-tamale schoolmarm. Fran's elderly nanny said that you and your Similac-breath, hotshot boy toy remind her of the slow jam 'Love You Down' by Ready for the World. Floppy's guardian said that no wonder Casper is hot for teacher because you're a dime piece with the total package: brains, personality, and beauty."

Sheet Cake pauses and says: "Charlotte's G-ma told Yingjie's G-pa that when she googled you, she discovered you're so old, you and your heartthrob sportsman should star in a *Cougar Town* spin-off sitcom and call it Jaguar Town. Yingjie's G-pa told Charlotte's G-ma that he didn't care how young your pick-of-the-litter loverboy is 'cause you're a jewel and gifted educator. Tiny's mom butted in and said that she sleeps easier knowing your young trainee is a consenting adult and you're not sitting in *teacher jail* accused of being a mocha Mary Kay Letourneau. I'm guessing that lady was a *good* teacher who did a *bad* thing." Opinionated passerby on a mobility scooter chimes in, "Hmm, that's putting it mildly!"

Sheet Cake resumes relaying statements: "Betty's stepdad said that you and your ballplaying trophy husband are the poster children for colorblind cougar couple. Mary Starlett's mama said that you're a chocolate purring cougar, your boy hubby is a vanilla man-cub, and your churrin are mulatto kittens. Ray Ray's single mom said that Cougarlicious is the only slot machine you and Vivica Fox play. Ponytail's daddy called you a MILF and said that if Ford brings back the Mercury Cougar, you'd be the spokeswoman. Lynn's single dad said that you preyed and pounced on your brawny roundballer by clawing him with your manicured paws 'cause he was the perfect cougar bait. I also heard a soccer mom say something about a cougar bite and a stay-at-home dad mentioned dusting off a John Cougar Mellencamp album. What's with all that 'cougar' talk?" Suddenly, Dr. O'Brien recalls a movie scene from *Win a Date with Tad Hamilton!* and utters: "Shake-a-doo! Sheet Cake, you absorbed so much, I may start calling you *Sponge* Cake."

Dr. O'Brien takes a moment to digest everything Sheet Cake told her. Afterward, teacher takes a deep breath and explains: "Schoolmarm is a degrading term for a lady schoolteacher who's too strict or behind the times. The insulting plaything and goofy geriatric statements were because at 40-something, I was courted by a 20-something superstar with a 9-figure max contract. Those cheeky feline comments were because my husband and I have a sizable age difference plus we have oodles of mixed kids."

Stevie's 50-something Canadian glamma tells Dr. O'Brien: "We're ladies of a certain age. I think you smitten kittens are the cat's meow. The way you two look at each other makes me believe y'all were a match made in heaven. Getting it right the first time is the be-all and end-all!"

On October 15, National Hispanic Heritage Month concludes with a field trip to a Latin art museum.

Mid-November, class attends a taping of *Are You Smarter Than a 5th Grader?* Group enjoys the game show while snacking on Smarties.

Before winter break, "Dr. George" Fischbeck and "Science Bob" Pflugfelder put on a show in the auditorium to promote January's science fair. Final act is übercool. Thomas Dolby plays an instrumental version of "She Blinded Me with Science" as Dr. O'Brien assists the two experts in a far-out group experiment.

Late January, B-Raid overhears Dr. O'Brien talking with an old-timer and a newcomer while he painstakingly scrapes gunk off his expensive kicks. He hears them discussing STEM scholarships for girls, parent-teacher conferences, standardized test scores, and other topics. B-Raid zooms them out until their conversation piques his interest. He overhears his teacher telling her co-workers: "Between Irish Marvel and me, one of us has a ring secret." The juicy news spreads like wildfire around campus.

Next day, Dr. O'Brien assures her students that B-Raid's story isn't fake news and promises they'll find out what's so classified on the last school day.

Chapter Two

Second Quarter

First Friday in February's Black History Month, civil rights activists Linda Brown and Ruby Bridges speak at a school assembly. Two weeks later, Al Sharpton is scheduled to visit Dr. O'Brien's class. Day before Al's visit, he reschedules as the date and time conflict with his hair appointment.

Third Tuesday in March's Irish-American Heritage Month, Dr. O'Brien's class interacts with a fifth class in Waterford, Ireland via Skype. Day afterward, her students chow down Irish tacos and Pistachio Delight. They also take home Clodagh McKenna's recipe for Irish soda bread and a St. Patrick's Day Potato from See's Candies.

Late March, Dr. O'Brien's students spike her morning Irish Breakfast Tea with crushed sleeping pills while she's distracted by a fight. When teacher returns to her desk, she notices white particles floating in her favorite mug. After that, teacher displays her game face and does her version of a pump-fake. She pretends to drink her beverage and pass out onto the floor. Seconds later, teacher says in her groggy voice: "The … ring … secret … is, and in her normal voice, she utters, "Busted!" Teacher gets up, bluffs the class with a sham cam, and sternly states: "Listen up! I don't have a teacher's pet. If nobody fesses up, I'll recommend suspension to the principal for everyone!"

Moments later, ringleader Kathy Rose confesses: "I'm a Belieber who got major Bieber Fever. Like baby, baby, baby, oh! If I don't tell, my daddy won't let me go to the Biebs' concert. Since we're caught red-handed on camera, it's not the same as being a tattletale. As a class, we agreed to a fake fight because I told them I heard the song 'Talking in Your Sleep' by The Romantics. It's about a somniloquist who tells secrets in her sleep. We're truly sorry. We just wanted to see if you'd blurt out a spoiler alert about the ring secret if you caught some Z's in class."

On April Fools' Day, nobody gets flour-bombed and no prankster plays a clever prank. The following evening is Open House. Before event ends, Dr. O'Brien announces: "My husband and I are rewarding the class for getting straight A's on their second report cards. We're going to see Irish Marvel's team battle it out at a matinee grudge match on Saturday, April 17. The once-in-a-lifetime gameday experience includes transportation to the arena in a 30-passenger Hummerzine, lunch at a soul food restaurant, VIP clubhouse tour, class interview during pregame show, game ball delivery by the class, courtside tickets, an Irish Marvel bobblehead, foam finger, and a signed team basketball for each padawan." Next, teacher passes out permission slips and draws six parent chaperone names from a raffle drum.

Irish Marvel is the face of the franchise. The 7-footer is a starter, captain, and plays the center position. His 14-season pro resumé includes being a nine-time all-star player and six championships.

Republican politician Herman Cain sings "The Star-Spangled Banner." Former Democratic president Bill Clinton accompanies the singer on tenor saxophone. After their riveting bipartisan performance, ring announcer, Michael Buffer, comically introduces two starting lineups and two head coaches. Mr. Buffer ends with his famous catchphrase.

First and second quarter of the matchup are fast-paced. Home team and visiting team are tied at the half. The halftime show is a death-defying circus act that literally has everyone sitting on the edge of their seats. Just before halftime ends, Dr. O'Brien's class of 11 schoolboys and 11 schoolgirls are stoked to see their names displayed on the Jumbotron as Fleetwood Mac's "Don't Stop" plays.

Female Classmates

Betty

Charlotte

Fran

Gracie

Kathy Rose

Lynn

Mary Starlett

Rebecca

Sheet Cake

Tiny

Valerie

Male Classmates

B-Raid

Dolf

Dreadhead

Floppy

Ponytail

Ray Ray

Rudy

Shakobe

Stevie

Superboy

Yingjie

Irish Marvel phenomenally scores 102 points at the end of the third quarter by shooting a buzzer-beater nearly 70 feet away from the bucket. Ralph Lawler, the legendary play-by-play announcer, stands up behind the score table, turns a cartwheel in his noggin, and zestfully articulates with every breath in his pulsating lungs: "Binnnnnnnnnnnnnnnnnnnnnnnnnnnnnnnnnnnnnnnnnnngo! Step aside Wilt, there's a new centurion in town named Marvin 'Irish Marvel' O'Brien!"

Ralph's broadcast partner, Mike Smith, who serves as color analyst, says: "Unbelievable! Are you kidding me? I think the clutch player must've started a new pre-game ritual of listening to Eddy Grant's 'Electric Avenue' 'cause that was electrifying! Somebody should call co-hosts Fran Tarkenton, Cathy Lee Crosby, and John Davidson to tell that threesome we just watched our own episode of *That's Incredible!*" Seconds later, Mike faints from sheer shock. A team dentist revives Mike with aromatherapy. Ralph teases Mike: "I didn't think you had a *mute* button." Being a good sport, Mike says: "There's a first time for everything, partner. You've seen those disgusting walrus whiskers on our head athletic trainer. I'm ecstatic I didn't need the kiss of life from *her* to start me up!"

Game clock stops after the fan favorite reaches the century mark. The arena makes an unprecedented move. Streamers and confetti that're always reserved for the end of a basketball game drop from the arena's ceiling. In the heat of the moment, Dr. O'Brien's students storm the court to make confetti angels. Shortly thereafter, cheerleaders perform to Kool & the Gang's "Celebration."

The juggernaut gets a standing ovation. Opposing team doesn't player hate while Deniece Williams' attaboy anthem "Let's Hear It for the Boy" plays. They congratulate by shaking the amped up player's hand. Afterward, he's interviewed briefly by Chris Broussard, Doris Burke, and Craig Sager. Next, his petite coach stands on her chair and plants a congratulatory kiss on his forehead.

Irish Marvel grins ear to ear like a Cheshire cat, leapfrogs his shrewd agent, and chest bumps every teammate. Triple-figure player fist bumps John Wooden, Drake, Apolo Anton Ohno, Venus and Serena, The Kissing Bandit, Mike Tyson, Don King, Jack Nicholson, Prinz von Anhalt, Michael Clarke Duncan, Charo, Cal Worthington, Paul Rodriguez, "Weird Al" Yankovic, Spike Lee, Prince Harry, N.W.A, the unifier, superfan Jimmy Goldstein, Stephen A. Smith, Skip Bayless, Common, Ed Young, Kurtis Blow, Kelly Ripa, Michael Strahan, Margaret Cho, Will.i.am, Pitbull, Berry Gordy, Dick Clark, Pharrell, Lindsay Lohan, Snoop, members of Kiss, Dr. Sanjay Gupta, Gary Coleman, Ringo Starr, Nelson Mandela, Rihanna, McDreamy and McSteamy, Bruno Mars, Taylor Swift, Molly Ringwald, Icy Blu, Tom Cruise, George Wallace, Carrot Top, Usain Bolt, Rob Fukuzaki, Whitney and Bobbi Kristina, Patrick Anderson, Soledad O'Brien, Hue Hollins, Penny Marshall, Billy Crystal, and Muhammad Ali.

The southpaw waves to a team beat writer and high-fives his wife's school group. Next, the kiss cam operator spotlights the super-size player and pint-size teacher. While Mickey & Sylvia's "Love is Strange" plays, the couple's passionate PDA lingers for a whopping 102 seconds. After the lovebirds' long-lasting lip-lock, they're given a thunderous applause.

Everyone is so engrossed in the excitement. No referee calls a delay-of-game penalty. As the atmosphere in the arena calms down, court is cleaned and spectators return to their seats. Fourth quarter begins and ends uneventfully. Lawler's Law rings true. Final tally is 143-128.

After the star-studded playoff ballgame, Dr. O'Brien finds a stat sheet underneath her seat. She writes 102 with violet lip gloss on the backside and gives it to her husband. *Sports Illustrated* takes a group photograph of Harvey Pollack, Mike, Ralph, day-trippers, and the shooting star holding that sign under the 10-foot goal where the history-making, three-point shot was netted. After that, the coach, owner, GM, Irish Marvel, a scout, longtime season-ticket holder, and 22 classmates carry out a college championship tradition by taking turns cutting down the net. Next, the team mascot sneaks up on the star performer for a Gatorade shower. That night, everyone watches the replay of the game. They hear Ralph and Mike's banter continue until the postgame show ends.

Two days later, Stuart "Boo-Yah" Scott visits Dr. O'Brien's class for a *SportsCenter* segment. Just as Stuart commences the story behind his famous catchphrase, "cooler than the other side of the pillow," class is interrupted by a life-saving nuisance – the fire drill. After returning to the classroom, Stuart finishes the story and wraps up by asking classmates: "Which was better, seeing the sold-out contest at home or watching it in person?" Students don't haggle. They unanimously agree that watching it on the boob tube was just as fun as the jaunt itself.

Three Saturdays thereafter, Irish Marvel's alma mater retires his high school basketball jersey No. 5.

Al Sharpton's visit is rescheduled for today, May 19. His visit gets cancelled at the eleventh hour because he's spearheading a demonstration about police brutality. Later that same day in another state, Al, Jesse Jackson, and Professor Dyson are slated to speak at a rally for slavery reparations.

Halftime Report

In terms of basketball quarters, you've reached the halfway mark. Take a break and resume when you're ready.

Chapter Three

Third Quarter

Today is Thursday, June 24, 2010, the last day of school. Eager kids have waited months for the shroud of secrecy to be lifted. Before class begins, Dr. O'Brien's students present her with two hand-painted Irish coffee mugs bought with their pooled allowances. Teacher thanks everyone.

Tardy bell rings. Dr. O'Brien says, "Good morning." Afterward, teacher plays the introduction to MiJac's "Wanna Be Startin' Somethin' " song. Next, she rings up the curtain on the fifth-grade promotion party with a yearbook DVD capturing Kodak moments.

Dr. O'Brien states: "Welcome to our Soul Train theme party." After that, she uncovers a disco ball hanging from the ceiling, unveils a replica of the Soul Train Scramble Board, and tells: "We'll use it as we take the hippest trip in America."

Minutes later, Mrs. Seward, the vice principal, and Principal Worm stop by to check out the bash. Mrs. Seward remarks: "This classroom looks like the set of *Soul Train*." Principal Worm asks Dr. O'Brien: "Is Don Cornelius coming to the shindig?" Teacher says: "The creator and longtime host of *Soul Train* isn't coming." Soon after, Principal Worm and Mrs. Seward dance down a soul train line, do the limbo, and then say, "Toodle-oo." Afterward, Irish Marvel's rookie teammate, Spencer, drops by on his way to visit Mr. Gorski's fourth-grade class. Player does the Dougie, Stanky Leg, Cha Cha Slide, and *Thriller* video dance with the class.

Dolf inquires: "Is Big Hunk gonna miss our party so he can score fast-break points and slam-dunk on national TV?" Dr. O'Brien answers: "The 2009-2010 pro basketball season is already in the books."

Shortly thereafter, Dr. O'Brien serves her blue-ribbon fruiggie smoothie during snacktime. As the party goes on, learners frolic outdoors and play fun indoor games. Later, teacher displays a life-size cardboard cutout of Al Sharpton apologizing and she distributes Al's gift bags. They contain backpacks filled with school supplies, lip whistles, board games, and Chia Pets.

Appetizing family-style lunch consists of garden salad, pizza, Irish nachos, spaghetti, and onion rings. Class eats vegan cupcakes with a 2010 ring topper for dessert. After devouring the toothsome goody, everyone licks the frosting off their toppers. Class washes their party favor rings and wears them.

Ten minutes later, Dr. O'Brien receives a text and announces: "The center of my universe just texted to say he'll be here momentarily." As the world-class cager enters the schoolroom with a dozen blue roses, rambunctious pupils pound their desk and chant, "Bliss Kiss!" After the umpteenth chant, Irish Marvel responds, "Not today."

Rebecca says: "Dr. O'Brien, you're wearing yellow, so ya gotta kiss your fellow." Irish Marvel jokes: "I dialed her heart and Soulja Boy told me to kiss her through the phone."

Dolf inquires: "Did you and Fighting Irish have a knock-down-drag-out and break each other's stuff like my parents did before they split the sheets 'cause they both scratched that seven-year itch and had affairs?" Dr. O'Brien says: "Neither of us bedmates made the IWAD-statement. We didn't leave our home this morning singing Fats Domino's 'Ain't That a Shame.' We're not leaving lovers' lane because of a lover's quarrel. I'm not a drama queen who abuses my husband by using him as a punching bag nor does Irish Marvel have that dreadful Ike Turner disease."

Tiny states: "I've heard stories about pimps and controlling pricks – grown men and teen boys – Ike-ing chicks. My cousin's college roomie, Missy, works at a battered women's shelter. Missy told me that domestic violence can be the other way around, but guys don't talk about it 'cause people will think they're wusses."

Irish Marvel informs: "I didn't get the silent treatment or sleep on the couch yesternight. We aren't going through a rough patch. We don't need to rekindle the romance. We aren't in rebuilding mode. We haven't separated legally or informally. We don't have hardball lawyers negotiating a buyout or deal to sign and trade our individual 'I do' for 'I'm dunzo!' There's no war-of-the-O'Briens divorce lockout. We're still role players who peacefully perform our duties as a married couple and purposeful parents. Marriage isn't always a bed of roses. We know how to keep our hands to ourselves when we lock horns. I didn't marry a battleax and *real* love isn't a battlefield. Home should always be a safe haven."

Kathy Rose states: "I'm totally confused. Y'all are like that old Hall & Oats song. Your kisses are on each other's list of the best things in life. If you or Hot Lips didn't do something turrible to deserve getting kicked to the curb and nobody had to pack a sh*t kit yesterday to stay somewhere else, then why no B.K. today?" Irish Marvel states: "Watch your language! Cusswords abuse God's gift of speech. The missus and I only pucker up on my *unannounced* visits." Relieved kids say, "Whew!"

Ray Ray comments: "On those unannounced visits, you and Lucky Lips always sucked face like that famous kissing couple on the cover of *Life* magazine. Every time, you two looked like y'all were ringing in the new year at midnight or celebrating Valentine's Day. Lady Gaga must have worn a Cupid costume to a Halloween party, saw y'all with two straws sharing a Funky Cold Medina, and shot you two in the heart with a bow and arrow so y'all would be forever gaga over each other." Dr. O'Brien says: "I can tell you that it wasn't Lady Antebellum or Lady of Rage rocking her afro puffs. The shooter was actually Grace Jones. She hit the bull's eye while we were dressed as Beauty and the Beast and doing the Monster Mash. Just kidding! Nor did we swig a bottle of Love Potion No. 9. Speaking of Cupid, that's our cue to do the Cupid Shuffle."

After everyone returns to their seats from doing the line dance, Valerie inquires: "Do people hafta use a GPS, try paper bag speed dating, attend a megachurch wearing their Sunday best, or dance on *Soul Train* in order to find a soul mate?" Dr. O'Brien tells: "The ancient Greek philosopher, Plato, introduced the concept of soul mates. Plato believed men and women were separated by Greek gods causing them to roam the earth in search of a perfect partner. The modern-day terms *other half* and *better half* are thanks to Plato's teaching. Having a soul mate isn't *real* but having a special someone *is*. That person should be a marriage partner for life who's inspired by God, yet motivated by love, to work together no matter what because he or she shares the same core values, priorities, and goals. Some pray they meet that person through their house of worship. Others look online. My paternal cousin, Dale, danced on *Soul Train* back in the 1970s. I know he had a whale of a good time, but I can't say that dancing on television helped him in the love department. That special someone can be found anytime at anywhere."

Tiny asks: "After you first gave each other some sugar, did either of y'all have a triple F?" Together couple reply, "What's a triple F?" Tiny says: "Flash forward fantasy. If there's a spark when getting to first base, right away you can picture your wedding, honeymoon, having crumb snatchers, and spending the rest of your life with that person. I heard about it last year from the *Flower Girl* chick flick on the Hallmark Channel when my friends Danielle, Brenda, Janice, Barbara, Esther, Lois, Malala, Little Tanya, Ashlyn, Sasha, Lauren, Flair, Alina, Jackie, Ila, Millie, Dashanna, Bessie, and I were kickin' it at my slumber party." Dr. O'Brien responds: "I heard a symphony, then I had a triple F, but I never told anybody." Irish Marvel says: "No chamber orchestra or symphony orchestra played in my head. I didn't know what it was called back then, but I definitely had one of those. I couldn't help myself. Like Sugar Pie Honey Bunch, I didn't tell a soul."

All of a sudden, Dr. O'Brien's students make a beeline for the window and go crazy. They witness Prince parking a convertible little red Corvette, applying guyliner, untying his rhinestone do-rag, and primping his permed hairstyle to perfection.

In the classroom, Prince sings "Diamonds and Pearls," performs a guitar solo of "Kiss," and brings the house down with "Baby I'm a Star." After the class parties like it's 1999, Prince counts to three and tosses Dr. O'Brien a raspberry beret. On his way out, Rudy asks: "Is the lion in your pocket ready to roar?" Prince answers: "Not today, kid. I didn't bring that finger puppet with me."

Soon after, class receives v-mail from Prince heading home to Paisley Park on his private jet. Video shows him wearing his ring topper, eating the last cupcake, and opining: "Best I've tasted in all of my purple life!"

Irish Marvel plays ABBA's "When I Kissed the Teacher." As it plays, Dr. O'Brien states: "Bliss Kiss Chart shows we had 14 make-out sessions. He and I did so without standing under any mistletoe. Shortest kiss happened the morning of Tuesday, September 29 when we smooched 10 seconds for my room number. Longest kiss occurred the afternoon of Friday, May 14 when we kissed 26 seconds for the English alphabet." Superboy notices the chart's top left kissing ball hanging slightly lower than the top right kissing ball and tells: "I remember that rainy day. Y'all looked like one of those hot-and-heavy cover couples on my grandmother's Harlequin romance novels."

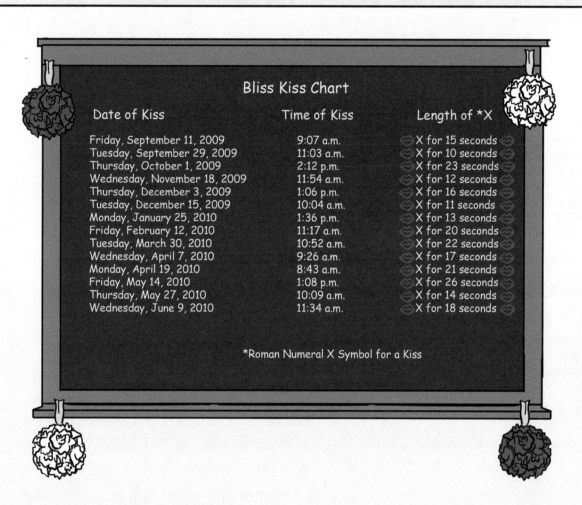

Bliss Kiss Chart

Date of Kiss	Time of Kiss	Length of *X
Friday, September 11, 2009	9:07 a.m.	X for 15 seconds
Tuesday, September 29, 2009	11:03 a.m.	X for 10 seconds
Thursday, October 1, 2009	2:12 p.m.	X for 23 seconds
Wednesday, November 18, 2009	11:54 a.m.	X for 12 seconds
Thursday, December 3, 2009	1:06 p.m.	X for 16 seconds
Tuesday, December 15, 2009	10:04 a.m.	X for 11 seconds
Monday, January 25, 2010	1:36 p.m.	X for 13 seconds
Friday, February 12, 2010	11:17 a.m.	X for 20 seconds
Tuesday, March 30, 2010	10:52 a.m.	X for 22 seconds
Wednesday, April 7, 2010	9:26 a.m.	X for 17 seconds
Monday, April 19, 2010	8:43 a.m.	X for 21 seconds
Friday, May 14, 2010	1:08 p.m.	X for 26 seconds
Thursday, May 27, 2010	10:09 a.m.	X for 14 seconds
Wednesday, June 9, 2010	11:34 a.m.	X for 18 seconds

*Roman Numeral X Symbol for a Kiss

Dr. O'Brien talks about a unique flowering plant called Psychotria Elata a.k.a. Hooker's Lips. Afterward, she shows a picture of it, passes out red candy lips, and asks: "Does anyone know the O-verb meaning to kiss?" Yingjie takes an educated guess and says, "Oscillate." Teacher responds: "You're close. *Oscillate* is a nine-letter verb describing how a fan swing. *Osculate* is an eight-letter verb meaning to kiss. FYI: Philematology is the study of kissing."

Dreadhead states: "Irish Marvel must use that ancient 'Kiss me, I'm Irish' tactic all the time. If you guys aren't prepping for a kiss-in protest or training to compete in a smooch-a-thon, Irish Marvel should get Dr. O'Brien's lips tatted on his neck like that power forward in Denver with the rapper girlfriend. That way, y'all don't hafta play kissy-face so much."

Irish Marvel explains: "Me and Sweet Pea snog a lot because kissing is an affectionate sign of deep respect, trust, and appreciation. Like milk, kissing your sweetheart does a body good. My wife's Cupid's bow on her top lip makes it hard for me *not* to want to kiss her luscious lips." Next, fifth graders look around the class to see who else has a Cupid's bow. Basketballer says: "Many moons ago, I kissed that tattoo idea goodbye. As big and strong as I am, I'm a fraidy-cat when it comes to needles. I would scream, visualize myself being blasted out of a cannon, and skedaddling like the Road Runner."

Dr. O'Brien asks: "By show of hands, how many know the Bible mentions tattoos?" All hands are down. Irish Marvel tells, "The Scripture is at Leviticus 19:28." Superboy states: "My godparents have matching tats. They never mentioned that God's Word talked about crayons for grown-ups."

Lynn inquires: "Why do married folks call each other 'rib'? Is it because they like to get their grub on by eating a gang of barbequed baby back ribs at a cookout?" Irish Marvel replies: "God created the first man, Adam, from dust on the ground. After an unknown period of time, God created the first woman, Eve, from one of Adam's ribs while he was sleeping. God did that so Adam would have a helper and companion. By Adam being a *man*, that's how we got the word *woman*."

Stevie asks, "Was Adam's six-pack lopsided?" Irish Marvel answers: "Adam's washboard abs were most likely unaffected when God closed up his flesh. Each side of a person's rib cage normally has 12 ribs. The Gloved One had an extra rib. FYI: Black lines on basketballs are called ribs."

Ponytail inquires, "Did Adam have a hideous scar?" Irish Marvel responds: "Nope. Our first parents, Adam and Eve, were head-to-toe perfect."

Dr. O'Brien asks: "How many have heard the legend that as the pair were being booted out the garden for punishment, Eve held a four-leaf clover to hold onto a little piece of paradise?" Some raise their hands to say that rings a bell. Teacher explains: "They disobeyed God's command not to eat from the tree of knowledge in the middle of the garden. Taking a souvenir wasn't allowed. The Bible book of Genesis, chapter three, tells that before the naughty two ate from God's tree, they walked around the Garden of Eden in the buff without knowing it. After eating the *nameless* forbidden fruit, they became aware of their nakedness. So, Adam and Eve sewed fig leaves together and made loin coverings. If they hadn't lost their home, Adam could've eaten from a second tree called the tree of life and lived forever. Because of their actions, we inherited imperfection and death."

Dolf inquires: "So, what's the dillio with the Adam's apple? Did Adam get a glob of apple fries stuck in his throat?" Irish Marvel says: "No. Laryngeal prominence is the real name for the dude bump. It protects the larynx a.k.a. voice box from injuries."

Ponytail asks: "Is it true Adam and Eve's children married each other and had kids?" Irish Marvel states: "God allowed it back then to populate the earth."

Dr. O'Brien introduces the couple's Native-American jeweler, Mr. Windfeather. Teacher gives their chum a cheek peck and her lulu. He puts her ring on the jewelry scale and exclaims: "The boulder weighs a ton!" Ray Ray says: "No way. One time, my funcles Ronnie, Odell, Lawrence, George, Van, and David took me and my homeboys, Big Glynn and Chicken Wayne, to the zoo. The zookeeper said that baby elephants can weigh a ton. Her ring can't be *that* heavy." Jeweler from the Gem State responds: "I was joking. The boy wearing the headband is right. A baby elephant can weigh 2,000 pounds, which is one ton. The jewels on her enormous eye-catcher only weigh 10,000 carats."

As the party evolves, most of the kids are fascinated with unscrambling activities on the Soul Train Scramble Board. Some pouting party-poopers ask: "How much longer before you tell the big secret?" Teacher says: "We'll keep it under wraps just a wee bit longer."

Fran inquires: "Is the ring secret about something spooky, time travel, bad karma, jewel heist, a royal and a poor commoner, passage to an enchanting place, a diary, tainted love, poetic justice, alien abduction, a Negro spiritual, Claddagh ring, a do-over, grab bag, ring-tailed lemur, tricky riddle, kick-butt shero, reincarnation, blackmail, a Banksy painting, deathbed confession, a promposal, sports equinox, a dilemma, pirates booty map, drone-spying, vampires, zombies, alternative fact, frenemies, stupendous stepgrandparents, anonymous pen pals, twisted twin, cyberhacker, a scandal, murder mystery, or El Chapo and Bin Laden's hideouts?" Dr. O'Brien responds, "Great guesses. It's none of the aforementioned."

Rudy asks: "Can you give a hint, clue, or tell us if the secret has a sad beginning with a happy ending, if there's a missing link or cliffhanger like my abuela's telenovelas?" Irish Marvel replies: "If you added pretty please with sugar on top, I'd still be tight-lipped."

Charlotte inquires: "What about that lingerie lady at the mall, General Petraeus, or the prez's road dawgs who hang out with him? You know … the Frank Farmer fellows with the twirly earpiece cord and cool wrist mic. Do any of them know?" Dr. O'Brien states: "Unlike Victoria's secret, our closely-guarded secret isn't for sale. General Petraeus and the Secret Service have bigger fish to fry and aren't privy to our secret."

Floppy speculates: "I think whatever the hush-hush is, it's something stashed inside one of Irish Marvel's Versace sportscoats, nine all-star rings, six championship rings, or two Olympic rings. Maybe it's about a bromance, a game-time decision, Harry Potter wizardry stuff, or top-secret X's and O's to win the title next season."

Rebecca comments: "I hope one of them has spidey-sense and a power ring like comic book superheroes."

Irish Marvel remarks: "One Irishism states: 'Three people can keep a secret, if two of them are dead.' We'll take the wraps off when it's just right. Until then, our lips are sealed. When it's revealed, it'll knock your socks off!"

Dr. O'Brien says: "We're now going to switch gears and review the lower anatomy." Dolf asks: "So, are we going to rewatch that animated movie with Dr. Dean Edell, Dr. Drew, Dr. Ruth, and the four docs from *The Doctors,* or that after school special with Howard Stern, Salt-N-Pepa, and that Playboy Bunny guy?" Teacher replies, "Nope."

Irish Marvel asks: "Are we playing Who Knew? like Kathie Lee and Hoda Woman from *The Today Show*?" Dr. O'Brien answers: "Today isn't Winesday Wednesday. We're having an oral pop quiz as a class."

Irish Marvel picks up the first flashcard set and asks: "What's the word for being born a girl or boy?" Class answers, "Gender." Basketballer asks: "What's the name of the private part that boys and men have which means tail in Latin and rhymes with tennis?" Class answers, "Penis." Basketballer asks: "If you were born a boy and have a penis, your gender is what?" Class answers, "Male." Basketballer asks: "What's the name of the hair patch that grows above and around the penis?" Class answers, "Pubic hair." Basketballer asks: "What's the name of the skin pouch a male has that hangs behind and below the penis?" Class answers, "Scrotum." Basketballer asks: "What's the name of the two round parts inside the scrotum's dual compartment nicknamed 'Ping and Pong' that rhymes with popsicles?" Class giggles and answers, "Testicles." Jeweler adds: "*Family jewels* is another term for those glands." Basketballer asks: "Which leathery, single-seed fruit, also called the alligator pear, is the Aztec word for testicles?" Class answers, "Avocados."

Dr. O'Brien picks up the second flashcard set and asks: "What's the name of the *outside* private part that girls and women possess which is shaped like the letter V?" Class answers, "Vulva." Teacher asks: "What's the name of the pea-size part at the front of the vulva?" Class answers, "Clitoris." Teacher asks: "What's the name of the hair patch that grows to cover the vulva?" Class answers, "Pubic hair." Teacher asks: "If you were born a girl and have a vulva, your gender is what?" Class answers, "Female." Teacher asks: "What's another word for gender?" Class answers, "Sex." Teacher asks: "What's the name of the opening females have between their legs that rhymes with china?" Class answers, "Vagina." Teacher asks: "What's the real name for both genders' private parts a.k.a. nether regions?" Class answers, "Genitals." Teacher asks: "Does anyone remember the Latin word for genitals?" Class answers, "Genitalia."

Irish Marvel picks up the third flashcard set and asks: "What's the name of the muscular sac that stores our pee until it's ready to be emptied?" Class answers, "Bladder." Basketballer asks: "Does anyone remember the real name for pee?" Class answers, "Urine." Basketballer asks: "What's the name of the tube that releases urine?" Class answers, "Urethra." Basketballer asks: "In males, where's the urethra located?" Class answers, "Inside the penis." Basketballer responds: "It's the hole at the end of the penis, right on the tip of the head." Teacher asks: "In females, is the urethra inside the vagina?" Class answers, "No." Basketballer explains: "Females urinate from the urethra which is *above* the vagina."

Dr. O'Brien picks up the fourth and final flashcard set and asks: "What's the name of the area where our legs meet the upper body?" Class answers, "Crotch." Teacher asks: "What's the name of the groove thing we were shaking earlier?" Class giggles and answers, "Buttock." Teacher asks: "What's the name of the muscle that shapes our bottoms?" Class answers, "Gluteus maximus." Teacher asks: "What's the real name for poop?" Class answers, "Feces." Teacher asks: "What's the name of our poop chute that rhymes with the planet Uranus?" Class answers, "Anus." Teacher asks: "What's the name of the area between our genitals and our anuses?" Class answers, "Perineum."

Teacher says: "Well done, boys and girls! Give yourselves a pat on the back. Everyone should know the basic proper names of our lower anatomy. Everybody should feel comfortable saying them aloud. Nicknames are fine as long as it's not something taboo."

After a three-pointer-contest brain break, Stevie asks: "Is it true some people are born with girl *and* boy parts?" Dr. O'Brien answers: "Yes. People born with both body parts used to be called hermaphrodite, androgynous, or half and half. Now, they're called intersex."

Mr. Windfeather inquires, "Can intersexes be birth parents?" Irish Marvel explains: "It depends. If an intersex has male and female parts of the reproductive system, that person generally can't reproduce, meaning make babies. Nevertheless, they can adopt. Sometimes an intersex has all-male or all-female *inside* body parts, but the *outside* genitalia is ambiguous, meaning unclear. In that situation, an intersex may be *fertile*, meaning able to make babies or *infertile*, meaning unable to make babies because of health challenges."

B-Raid asks, "What's with those weird gender symbols?" Irish Marvel answers: "The *Mars* symbol with a circle and right-pointed arrow represents a *male*. The *Venus* symbol with a circle and cross below represents a *female*. Those symbols and the Shakespearean phrase *star-crossed lovers* stem from astrology."

Chapter Four

Fourth Quarter

Dr. O'Brien drops a bombshell: "Our family ball club comprises of a head coach, an assistant coach, and 12 teammates. We got enough small fry to make an Olympic basketball team for Coach K." All but one student responds, "Wowee!" Ray Ray asks: "Straight up or is that a tall tale?" Teacher answers: "I couldn't be any more straight up if I were Paula Abdul."

B-Raid says: "My gut tells me that one or both of you came as a package deal like the Brady Bunch and later had some kids together." Irish Marvel replies: "No categorized kids … yours, mine, and ours. So, no mini-mes from previous relationships, on-break babies, stepchildren, or side kids." Dr. O'Brien remarks: "For *me*, being a second wife and/or stepparent were non-negotiables."

Betty asks: "Do you two have a rainbow tribe of adopted kiddies like that topless, banana-wearing entertainer, Josephine Baker?" Dr. O'Brien answers: "We don't have adoptees or foster children. Nor are we providing kinship care. Team O'Brien isn't a blended family."

Rebecca says: "I heard babies come from White Storks, cabbage patches, and watermelon seeds." Next, Dr. O'Brien pulls out a DVD from her desk entitled *Where Do Babies Come From?* and tells: "It'll explain everything." After the DVD conks out, teacher says "darn it" and informs: "Traditionally, babies are made from a loving *adult* activity called sexual intercourse or sex for short. Babymaking music is optional. Babies can happen whether a man and woman are married or single. To conceive, meaning to make a baby, a male has to put his erect penis inside a female's vagina so that his sperm can swim to her ovum a.k.a. egg. FYI: It doesn't look like an egg in the fridge or a Cadbury Cream Egg. The word *erect* means the pituitary gland inside the brain has sent a chemical message to the penis to change its appearance. Blood flow causes the penis to become bigger, rigid, and point up to easily fit inside the vagina the same way a key fit a lock. Hundreds of sperm will *reach* the ovum, but only one will *enter* the ovum."

Stunned students continue listening as Irish Marvel explains: "The joining process is called fertilization. A fertilized ovum is called a *zygote*. The zygote grows to form an *embryo*. An embryo is what an unborn child is called until the end of eight weeks of life. At nine weeks until birth, the unborn child is called a *fetus*. The fetus grows in a female's uterus a.k.a. womb for a little more than nine months. The uterus is inside the lower stomach just below the female's navel a.k.a. bellybutton. When the fetus is ready for birth, the vulva and vagina stretch like a rubber band to push the fetus out. The vagina is also called the birth canal."

Dr. O'Brien tells: "If vaginal birth isn't the best option for mother and child, a doc will do a surgical birth called a Caesarean section a.k.a. C-section. The scheduled or emergency surgery is done by cutting a small opening across the female's lower stomach to remove the fetus and close the uterus with stitches."

Floppy says: "Yikes! I see why my squeamish dad passed out in the delivery room. So, did a lady or man invent sex?" Irish Marvel answers, "*God* invented sex."

Yingjie says: "Sex is gross! I can't believe people like to get butt naked just to go half on a baby. Does doing it hurt?" Dr. O'Brien tells: "Sex is a private gift of self that's meant to be pleasurable and fun. 'Doing it' shouldn't cause either partner to fill out an Ouch Report. In fact, sex can be part of a normal pregnancy and it won't harm the babe. The *primary* purpose of sex is to cement married couples on three levels: spiritual, emotional, and physical. Going half on a baby is a *secondary* purpose."

Fran asks: "Is it true that you-know-what can be bad?" Irish Marvel responds: "Yes. Bad sex is rarely about someone's equipment or technique. It's usually about a lack of communication or something troubling one or both partners. People use the lame excuse - what if the sex is bad - to justify having sex before marriage."

Mary Starlett says: "S-E-X is totally oogie! It's worse than sulfur burps, foul farts, eating boogers, catching cooties, and mooning someone. When I grow up, I'm never, ever going to play hide the summer sausage! Is there such a thing as marriage without S-E-X?" Irish Marvel replies: "A marriage is considered S-E-X-less if a couple 'play hide the summer sausage' less than 10 times a year. Some couples have a white marriage, meaning they never had S-E-X from jump street. At your age, having S-E-X sounds really Y-U-C-K-Y. If you marry when you're an adult, you'll feel really L-U-C-K-Y to have it."

Gracie says: "Grown-ups should have somebody to love, especially those allergic to pets. So, what's the big stink about gay marriage?" Irish Marvel explains: "Who you love *romantically* matters to God. Same-sex marriage boils down to votes during election years and economic benefits. Marriage equality supporters think it's okay for *lawmakers* to redefine marriage. Whatever happens law-wise, remember, no court ruling will ever change *God's* definition of marriage."

Dr. O'Brien says: "Being gay isn't the new normal. By show of hands, how many have heard of Sodom and Gomorrah?" Some hands go up. Teacher tells: "Sodom and Gomorrah were the first gay communities. God eradicated those cities with rain made of sulfur and fire. Our Creator designed the blueprint for family life. God did it for heterosexuals, meaning people attracted to the opposite gender. Marriage wasn't meant for two wives or two husbands. The kids may be all right in that modern family, but two lesbian moms or two gay dads violate God's *balanced* family plan. Just because God hasn't obliterated any cities lately doesn't mean the design has changed or is outdated. Also, God didn't create Miriam and Steve so that Adam and Eve could be bisexual, meaning attracted to both genders."

Fran has a light-bulb moment and says to herself: "So, that's what Mrs. Tanaka meant. *Bi* is short for bisexual." Fran recalls the time when she and her mom ran into their skinny-dipping neighbor, Mrs. Tanaka, who they hadn't seen in months. When Fran's mom saw Mrs. Tanaka at the concession stand before a powderpuff football game, she asked her how she was doing. Mrs. Tanaka reacted by breaking into the ugly cry and said that her arranged marriage to Mr. Tanaka was a farce because he's bi. Mrs. Tanaka also said that she discovered her trifling-a** husband had been having a roll in the hay for 17 years with some Pakistani polo player. During halftime, Fran's mom and Mrs. Tanaka continued chatting about her *Brokeback Mountain* nightmare. After the game, Fran's mom told Fran that she shouldn't worry about Mrs. Tanaka because she's now happily divorced and attending veterinary school.

Irish Marvel says: "Nobody is born gay. There's no gay gene. If a person has romantic feelings for someone in a way that God disapproves and *wants* to change; that person can seek spiritual help, join a support group, practice self-control, or choose not to be romantically involved with anybody. No one should be mistreated because of your opinion about gay people. Nobody should be slurred or bullied for their sexual orientation whether their choice is out in the open or in the closet. Being homophobic won't get you any cool points and it can get you in big trouble at school, home, work, and with the police."

Dr. O'Brien remarks: "There's no coming-of-age or rite-of-passage excuse for premarital sex and making babies. Sex outside of a man-and-woman marriage is wrong because it breaks the Originator's rule, misuses the genitals, and trashes the precious gift. Sex-wise, true love and traditional marriage should always come before a baby carriage." The lyrics to the "K-I-S-S-I-N-G" children's song emerges on the overhead projector and class starts singing using the couple's names.

Rudy gets a puzzling look on his face and inquires: "If marriage is only supposed to be between one man and one woman, then what the heck is an open marriage?" Irish Marvel tells: "It's a hall pass for married individuals to play the field, which defeats the purpose of marriage. A tried-and-true marriage is practicing monogamy, meaning having one sex partner at a time. Permission or not, being married is like playing Monopoly; you get one token otherwise it's cheating."

Dr. O'Brien says: "Every grown-up isn't dating, courting, engaged, or married. Some are single by *choice*. Others are single by *chance*. Being a partnerless person isn't all doom and gloom. Singleness is a gift of time and freedom to live life as you see fit. Married with children is admirable, but it's not the only path to a long and happy life. Individuals, whether young or old, married or chronically single, should have the same goal, which is to live their best lives."

Stevie asks: "Can a seed planter man up by draining his dragon on a stick to see if he knocked up his bae?" Irish Marvel responds: "K.U. is offensive slang. Baby news may be a miracle, surprise, or even a wake-up call to turn someone's life around, but it's never an accident or a mistake. God has a purpose for each pregnancy. A female pee-pees on a test stick that comes with a home pregnancy test. The purpose is to see if the hormone called human chorionic gonadotropin (HCG) is present in her pee. The test result will be positive if a baby is brewing or negative if a baby isn't on the way. A seed planter could syphon his python on the stick since HCG could signal testicular cancer. However, there's no preg-dar for penis partners when they impregnate their vagina partners. The 'man up' part comes when the DNA blood test or DNA swab test inside the mouth cheek proves paternity. FYI: EPT sold the first U.S. home pregnancy test in 1978."

Valerie inquires: "So, how'd Pregnant Man get three real babies to grow in his man-oven?" Irish Marvel explains: "He's not related to a male seahorse. By that I mean, the guy doesn't have a pouch that allows him to carry and birth babies. Pregnant Man is a transperson a.k.a. transgender. When somebody is transgender, it means that person identifies himself/herself as the *opposite* of his/her birth gender. Transgenders feel they were born in the wrong body."

Mr. Windfeather remarks: "Back in the day when TV and water were free, we referred to somebody like that as she-male, he-she, or shim." Dr. O'Brien recalls the transperson tragically connected to singer Teddy Pendergrass and replies: "Those terms are offensive. Many people don't agree with a transgender's decision not to accept their God-given gender. Still, we should be respectful of their gender identity."

Irish Marvel says: "Pregnant Man isn't a medical mystery or some sideshow act. He's a *transman*, meaning a female-to-male transperson. It's also possible to be a *transwoman*, meaning a male-to-female transperson. Like Cher's son, Chaz, he was born a female. Pregnant Man changed his name from Tracy LaGondino to Thomas Beatie. Hormone injections helped him grow facial hair. He had *top* surgery above the waist to change his external appearance to male. The so-called Pregnant Man didn't have *bottom* surgery below the waist to change his internal female plumbing. He used donated sperm bought from the Internet."

Rebecca asks: "So, how'd sperm get inside the male mother's hoo-ha?" Irish Marvel sums it up with two words, "Turkey baster."

Ponytail inquires: "Which restroom does a transgender use if he or she only gotta do number one?" Dr. O'Brien answers: "Depending on the law, transgenders use what matches their *outward* gender presentation or use a unisex restroom."

Irish Marvel says: "Speaking of appearance, Deuteronomy 22:5 in the Bible tells us that cross dressing, meaning opposite-gender dressing, is something God detests."

Rebecca comments: "I wonder if God plays rocks-paper-scissors with the angels in heaven or use 'Eeny, meeny, miny, moe' to pick a baby's gender." Dr. O'Brien replies: "God blesses biological fathers with the gift of *gender* and blesses biological mothers with the gift of *birth*. The baby's sex is chosen at the finish line by the winner of a spectacular swim race inside a female's body, which is far more creative than any hand game or nursery rhyme."

Irish Marvel informs: "Humans are made from 46 rod-shaped cells that look like the letters X and Y. Males and females have 22 XY pairs of cells called autosomes, which are non-sex chromosomes. Every pair has one autosome from each parent. These cells give us our eye color, hair color, size, skin color, blood type, and gender. The 23rd cell is unique because it's the only *single* one. It waits to see if it's going to pair up with an X or Y. The 23rd cell is called the sex chromosome because it reveals the *sex* of a baby."

Dr. O'Brien illustrates a sex chromosome diagram. Using a pointer, she explains: "The female's ovum, which looks like a Vitamin E softgel, *always* carries the X chromosome. The male's wiggly sperm, which looks like a tadpole a.k.a. baby frog, *either* carries the X or Y chromosome."

Irish Marvel informs: "If the male's sperm with an X chromosome enters the female's ovum first, the baby will be a *girl* with XX chromosomes. If the male's sperm with a Y chromosome enters the female's ovum first, the baby will be a *boy* with XY chromosomes. Female X sperm are *slow*, but *strong* swimmers. Male Y sperm are *fast*, but *weak* swimmers. Ova a.k.a. eggs, both types of sperm and chromosomes are all teeny-weeny. They can only be seen under a powerful microscope."

Dr. O'Brien gives the females white T-shirts with **XX** letters while Irish Marvel gives the males white T-shirts with **XY** letters. Students remove their lab coats and don their T-shirts. Immediately, teacher realizes a photo opportunity has presented itself. So, she catches Mr. Marrow, the custodian, in the corridor to capture the moment.

Floppy says: "How does sperm build up energy to swim? I know they don't eat Wheaties Fuel to score points in the paint and prevent egg turnovers." Irish Marvel replies: "At the peak of sex, there's a happy grand finale. The technical name is orgasm, but grown folks often call it the big O."

Ponytail says: "I heard church ladies at my mom's hair salon mention the big O. I knew it wasn't about the retired point guard, the tire store, or the Ferris wheel in Tokyo. I just thought they were talking about Oprah's big *O* mag. Boy oh boy, was I way off the seesaw!"

Irish Marvel explains: "During the less-than-one-minute big O, both genders undergo a muscle tightening around their nether regions and feel a happy wave of body tingles. During a male orgasm, the spinal cord signals the penis to release a white fluid called semen. The process is called ejaculation. When that process happens, semen a.k.a. baby gravy, flows from the erect penis to feed and protect sperm. Semen and sperm travel together as a crew of two like Batman and Robin. One theory is that a female orgasm sucks up sperm into the uterus to assist with babymaking."

Irish Marvel refers to a teacher's edition textbook and illustrates a visual aid. Using a pointer, he explains a three-part sperm diagram: "The *head* carries the chromosomes. The *midpiece* contains a sugar called fructose. The fructose energizes the *tail* to journey to the ovum."

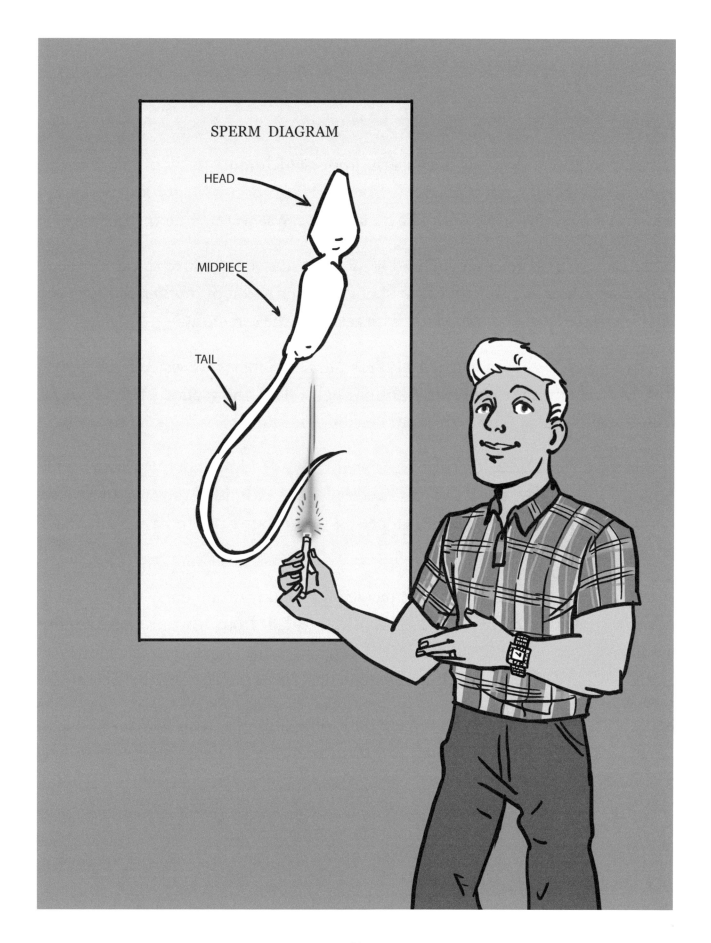

Ray Ray inquires: "So, how does sperm know which route to swim to get to the ovum?" Irish Marvel says: "They ask Michael Phelps or use MapQuest. Seriously, heat and the ovum's scent work like a navigation system to guide the sperm."

Lynn asks, "Isn't there a sex soup?" Dr. O'Brien answers: "You're thinking about *consommé,* which is a thin and clear soup. One definition of *consummate* is that a legal marriage has been completed with sex after the ceremony."

Rudy inquires: "Is it true married jailbirds can have jungle love visits in the joint?" Irish Marvel hums the chorus to Akon's "Locked Up" and replies: "Yep. *Conjugal* visits are allowed at some correctional facilities for inmates with good behavior."

Gracie asks: "Isn't there another sex related C-word? I know that it rhymes with halibut." Irish Marvel says: "I never heard it phrased with fish, but you're right. The C-word is *celibate*, which describes a person who chooses not to have sex because of religious or personal reasons."

Mary Starlett inquires: "Can a lad's pickle be too puny or too horsy to fit inside a lady's va-jay-jay?" Dr. O'Brien tells: "On average, lads from North Korea have the smallest pickles, whereas lads from the Congo have the biggest pickles. However, a lady's pickle jar is expandable and designed to fit all pickle sizes and shapes."

Betty asks: "Why do gray boys have pink ding-a-lings?" Irish Marvel answers: "That's an uncomplimentary term for Caucasian males. Penis color is usually a hereditary gift from dear ol' dad."

Sheet Cake inquires, "What's God's gender?" Irish Marvel tells: "God is a spirit, not a human being."

Dolf asks: "Who made God and why the name 'The Man Upstairs'?" Irish Marvel answers: "God wasn't created. 'TMU' is a heavenly nickname. The Bible states at Psalms 83:18 that God's name in English is Jehovah." Fran says: "Now, I get why Jay-Z calls himself J-Hova, the *god* of rap."

Valerie comments: "I knew that about God's name, but I wonder why people don't use it." Dr. O'Brien responds: "God is invisible. People can't put a face with the name. Imagine if people went around calling us by our gender instead of our names. That'd hurt our feelings."

Superboy says: "I'm bewildered. I know Jesus wasn't adopted from an agency in Bethlehem. So, how'd the Sky Guy make a son without a winkie, wifey, and getting busy?" Irish Marvel explains: "Jesus' *imperfect* mother was a virgin named Mary. Jehovah fertilized her ovum by Holy Spirit. Jesus was conceived while Mary was engaged to marry Joseph. Jesus was the last perfect person."

Kathy Rose inquires: "Why didn't Jehovah have a perfect daughter? She could've been a great teacher like her big bro and ran a princess charm school." Dr. O'Brien replies: "Only our heavenly Father knows. Although it would've been swell to be known as the world's only perfect siblings."

Mr. Windfeather comments: "My barber, Gregory, said that Adam, Eve, and Jesus didn't have a navel because they were perfect. If that's accurate, no navel piercing." Irish Marvel states: "The Bible doesn't say. If they had an innie or outie, I can't picture any of them wearing a belly ring."

Stevie says: "You look more like a sorority sister than a mega mom. Did you go under the knife for a mommy makeover to get plastic fantastic, workout at Curves, or use a stair gate to stay a brick house?" Momshell tells: "I didn't struggle with pregorexia. Nor did I get a breast lift and tummy tuck or use a *surrogate*. A surrogate – paid or unpaid – carries, gives birth, and hands over the newborn to a waiting person or couple. All of our flesh-and-blood gifts were delivered *by* me not *to* me."

Irish Marvel informs: "Third-party reproduction – sperm donors, egg donors, surrogates - are assisted ways to conceive babies. Baby batter suppliers, egg givers, and womb renters give up their rights to be parents even though they help bring children into the world."

Charlotte tells: "My boozy, loose-lipped gammy said that my homeschooled cuz's last name is a number 'cause my aunt ordered the daddy of her designer baby from a catalog after she gave her lazy live-in BF the marry-me-or-else ultimatum and he refused to make an honest woman of her." Dr. O'Brien clarifies: "If an anonymous egg donor or anonymous sperm donor is used, the donor's name isn't provided. The child may never know the identity of the bio-mom or the bio-pop's last name. In a nutshell, people need to R-E-S-P-E-C-T God's fertility plan. Making and birthing babies should only be done with one's spouse. Kids weren't designed to have multiple parents: an egg mom, a tote mom, a raised-me mom, or a seed dad and a raised-me dad. Adoption is a noble backup plan."

Yingjie remarks: "Sherman, my bonehead cousin away at boarding school in China, says that adoption is a fake forever family for those who don't mind taking in other people's abandoned kids from broken homes." Irish Marvel comments: "Perhaps to outsiders it may *seem* that way, but to ado-moms and ado-pops their families don't *feel* that way."

Dr. O'Brien says: "By the big 4-0, I wasn't married, divorced, widowed, an aunty, a godparent, or a mom. People assumed I felt left on the shelf, behind my peers, like a failure, incomplete, less than, empty, dead inside, or forgotten by God. They also assumed I was cursed, being punished for my past, a lipstick lesbian, bossy control freak, cynical, successful career woman married to my job, cheapskate, ice queen, faultfinder, too independent, she-devil, hermit, jaded, bitter, cuckoo, come from a dysfunctional family, didn't wanna be tied down, *sick of* kids, didn't *want* kids, couldn't *have* kids, lacked maternal instincts, had daddy issues, selfish, ratchet, had an awful childhood, shy, high-maintenance, feared rejection, too picky, had bad credit, needy, pining for the guy that got away, don't cook, discouraged, sheltered, couldn't keep a man, had philophobia, too set in my ways, carrying a torch for a bloke, a hot mess, worried about what-ifs, damaged goods, or a lost cause. All those something-must-be-wrong-with-me thinkers were off base. I always envisioned being a ma and grandma. I was just an eternal optimist trusting God's timing as to when to send me a two-in-one." Kids ask, "Don't you mean *the one*?" Teacher answers: "That's someone who'd be a good mate. *Two-in-one* is someone who'd be a good mate *and* good parent. We wanted to hear pitter-patter of tiny feet ASAP. When I birthed quadruplets at 47 in 2001, we torpedoed the maybe-she's-barren-and-maybe-he's-sterile theory. Quadruplets a.k.a. quads are four fetuses born during one birth. Fily, Viqy, Dixy, and Zigy are nimble nine-year-olds nicknamed 'The Gold Set.' "

Irish Marvel says: "My wife got a new wedding ring for our second wedding anniversary in 2001. The 5,000-carat ring had a heart-shaped sapphire in the center plus 4 diamonds. Around 9:30 a.m. that sunny morning, she was surprised to find it in a music box inside a sand sculpture on the private luxury island of Musha Cay in The Bahamas. Upon returning home, we celebrated further by sharing a colossal carrot cupcake. Five carrots were decorated around the side. Top center was adorned with a large diamond ring plus 5 and three 0 number candles. Below the candles was the writing: How Sweet It Is to Be Loved by You."

Mr. Windfeather asks: "Before y'all teamed up, did you two have a cradle list?" Irish Marvel answers: "Neither of us had a to-do list of accomplishments before parenthood."

Stevie inquires: "So, can people purchase sperm and extra eggs at Babies "Я" Us?" Dr. O'Brien says: "No. Jehovah created our bodies with built-in banks to kick in after puberty. Puberty is when the bodies of boys and girls change to look like grown-ups. It's also when people can activate their babymaking sex machines. Puberty usually happens at 8-13 for girls and 9-14 for boys. However, it'll happen when it's the right time for each person's body. Sperm production starts at puberty and stops at death. Sperm is made and stored inside the male's walnut-size testicles. Females are born with a lifetime egg supply. Our eggs mature at puberty. The 1-2 million eggs are stored in the female's almond-size ovaries. Each side of the uterus has one ovary. *Fertile* females ovulate once a month. When a female ovulates, it means the pituitary gland inside the brain has sent a chemical message for an ovary to release one egg from a small sac called a follicle. Hyperovulation happens when two or more eggs are released during one cycle." Next, teacher shows human ovulation pictures from the Net.

Shakobe asks, "How can fraternal twins have different dads?" Irish Marvel says: "That's possible if the mom hyperovulated two eggs and within 24 hours had congress with two men. FYI: DNA-wise, identical twins are 100 percent related. Whole siblings, DNA-wise, are 50 percent related and share *two* sets of grandparents. Half-siblings, whether they're uterine siblings (same mother) or agnate siblings (same father), DNA-wise, are 25 percent related and share *one* set of grandparents. As a result, some families have half-uncles, half-aunts, half-nieces, half-nephews, and half-cousins."

Dreadhead inquires: "What happens to the sperm and egg if they don't hit it off?" Irish Marvel explains: "Sperm may live inside the female's body for 3-7 days to marry up with an egg. If fertilization doesn't happen, sperm will be absorbed in the female's body. If one egg doesn't hit it off with one sperm within 24 hours after ovulation, it'll melt."

Mr. Windfeather asks: "Isn't menstruation the same thing as a menstrual cycle?" Dr. O'Brien replies: "No. A *menstrual cycle* has three phases and normally spans 28-35 days. *Menstruation*, commonly called a period or Aunt Flow, is phase one. It happens because an egg wasn't fertilized. During menstruation, the melted egg comes out and the endometrium sheds. Endometrium is a thick lining in the uterus for a baby. The shedding causes blood to flow from the vagina for an average of 3-7 days. Follicular phase is second. Around day 14, ovulation happens. Ovulation occurs at the end of the follicular phase. Luteal phase is third. It's the 12-16 days between ovulation and day one of a new cycle."

Charlotte says: "I heard boys have wet dreams so they can have kids when they're grown." Irish Marvel tells: "A nocturnal emission a.k.a. wet dream is nighttime sperm leakage that starts during puberty. It isn't necessary to make babies. In fact, all males don't have them. It's just a way to get rid of extra sperm."

Mr. Windfeather inquires: "Is it true a woman can pee on a stick to see when she'll ovulate?" Dr. O'Brien says: "Yes. She can purchase an ovulation predictor test kit and tinkle on a test stick daily at home. The purpose is to detect a surge of the egg releasing chemical called luteinizing hormone. After the first positive test, a *fertile* female should ovulate within 12-36 hours."

Dr. O'Brien erases the whiteboard and informs: "In 2004, when I was 49, I bore four more. Our spirited six-year-olds are Lacy, Wavy, Katy, and Mapy. That cluster clinched our elite eight. Keeping the Olympic theme, our second unit is nicknamed 'The Silver Set.' "

Irish Marvel tells: "I upgraded the gems on her wedding ring to 7,500 carats for our fifth wedding anniversary in 2004. It had a heart-shaped sapphire in the center plus eight diamonds. I surprised my wife with the jewelry during the indoor gondola ride at The Venetian in Las Vegas. We bussed under a bridge and I showed her the ring. At that moment, a minor earthquake rattled the gondola and it fell into the lagoon. A Good Samaritan, who's a Mr. T impersonator, found the ring and returned it. Again, upon returning home, we celebrated further by sharing a colossal carrot cupcake. Seven carrots were decorated around the side. Top center was adorned with a large diamond ring plus 7, 5, and two 0 number candles. Again, below the candles was the writing: How Sweet It Is to Be Loved by You."

Dr. O'Brien says: "Sperm and ovum can be fertilized outside a woman's body. True or false?" Class answers, "False." Teacher responds: "True. Traditionally, children are conceived through *in vivo fertilization*, meaning *inside* the body or naturally. Some kids are conceived nontraditionally through *in vitro fertilization*, meaning *outside* the body or artificially. With in vitro fertilization, sperm and ovum make a love connection, without the assistance of Chuck Woolery, on a Petrie dish at a laboratory. After three to five days, the girl or boy embryo of choice is transferred into a woman's uterus to attach to the lining and grow until birth. IVF babies are sometimes called test-tube babies. FYI: You can't tell by looking at a person whether he or she was conceived naturally or artificially."

Irish Marvel states: "Sometimes people have extra embryos after undergoing IVF. Some parents of leftover embryos decide their fam is complete and give up those remaining embryos for adoption. Children resulting from embryo adoptions are often called snowflake babies due to their frozen start."

Mary Starlett inquires: "Why do ladies have to go on a preconceive diet before they're in the family way?" Dr. O'Brien says: "A *preconception* lifestyle gets women and men into babymaking shape to increase the likelihood of conceiving a healthy baby."

Ray Ray asks: "Is it like the pro's preseason training camp or preparing for the Olympics?" Irish Marvel responds: "No. Good nutrition, fitness, and healthy living are usually enough to get folks into babymaking shape. Females get 90 days to improve their egg quality. Males get 100 days to improve their sperm quality."

Rudy inquires: "What does the F-word gotta do with nookie?" Dr. O'Brien explains: "It's a vulgar expression for sexual relations."

Tiny asks: "So, what does being a mom hafta do with the F-word?" Irish Marvel replies: "People say 'mother (bleep)-er' to vulgarly express an unpleasant thing or person."

Floppy inquires: "Do adults have to sing Rod Steward's 'Do Ya Think I'm Sexy?' or knock boots to be sexy?" Irish Marvel answers: "Nope. Being sexy isn't about being promiscuous, meaning having multiple sex partners at random. Grown folks do not have to be a slut or a stud. It's also not about a woman looking like a Hooters waitress or a man looking like a Chippendale dancer."

Rudy tells Ray Ray: "My godmom doesn't mind going to Hooters since my godpop can't see those hot Hooter Girls because he's blind as a bat." Ray Ray tells Rudy: "My daddy ordered Hooters famous chicken wings from their takeout menu once. They were pretty tasty."

Valerie tells Sheet Cake: "I remember seeing those shirtless Chippendale dancers on *The View* when I was sick as a dog two years ago with the stomach flu on Valentine's Day. I thought those buff, bowtie-wearing dancers with matching cuffs looked more like cute personal trainers." Sheet Cake tells Valerie: "I wanna know what kinda dance crew they are." Valerie sneezes and tells Sheet Cake: "Beats me. I've watched every episode of *America's Best Dance Crew* and they were never on that show. Maybe they missed the audition."

Irish Marvel says: "Getting back to Floppy's question … to be grown and sexy, adults just need a friendly smile, self-confidence, positive attitude, and the ability to hold a decent convo."

Mr. Windfeather realizes he has his wife's phone. Shortly thereafter, it rings. Everyone laughs because her ringtone for him is Right Said Fred's "I'm Too Sexy."

Dr. O'Brien tells: "In 2007, when I was 52, our household expanded fourfold for the third time. Our thriving three-year-olds are Nury, Judy, Huey, and Quby. Continuing with the Olympic theme, our third unit is appropriately nicknamed 'The Bronze Set.' You-know-who wears jersey No. 34 in honor of our triple-header quad squad."

Irish Marvel says: "I upgraded the gems on her wedding ring to 10,000 carats for our eighth wedding anniversary in 2007. The rock-around-the-clock ring she's wearing has 12 diamonds and a heart-shaped sapphire in the center. I surprised her with it while we were attending a luncheon at Le Jules Verne restaurant located on the second floor inside the Eiffel Tower in Paris. The center stone is her birthstone. Like a mother's ring, the diamonds around the sapphire represent the 12 children in our nuclear family. All our butterscotch babies were born in April. Their birthstone is the transparent mineral."

Mr. Windfeather informs: "There are four *precious* stones: diamond, emerald, sapphire, and ruby. The rest are *semiprecious* stones."

Irish Marvel says: "As usual, upon returning home, we celebrated further by sharing a colossal carrot cupcake. Ten carrots were decorated around the side. Top center was adorned with a large diamond ring plus 1 and four 0 number candles. Again, below the candles was the writing: How Sweet It Is to Be Loved by You."

Shakobe inquires: "What's with the threepeat carrot cupcakes?" Pointing to the teacher's super-duper sparkler, prolific pair answer, "*Carrot* for all the *carats*."

Yingjie asks: "Did you breastfeed all of your ankle-biters?" Dr. O'Brien responds: "Yes. They were exclusively breastfed two at a time for the first six months. Afterward, each quad set was bottle-fed breast milk along with some pureed, solid, and finger foods. After their first birthday, they continued eating table food and drank expressed breast milk from a cup until they reached their terrific twos."

Mr. Windfeather says: "I heard adoptive mommies can suckle their chosen ones. How's that possible?" Multipara answers: "Adoptive breastfeeding is possible through induced lactation. Even a nullipara, meaning a female who's never given birth, can produce milk for her adoptee or surrogate bundle of joy."

Dolf says: "I know dudes *without* man boobs can get breast cancer. Can dudes *with* man boobs breast-feed?" Irish Marvel explains: "There've been reported times when men *without* moobs have breast-fed infants because of herbs, medication, hormone shots, a brain tumor, starvation, mother's poor health, or the mom died."

Superboy asks: "What if the dairy queens are totally fake, pierced, and look like two footballs?" Dr. O'Brien answers: "Breast size doesn't matter. Birth mothers and instant moms can nurse their nurslings with natural breasts, implants, and pierced nipples. They may also employ wet-nurses or get a prescription for donor breast milk."

Ponytail asks: "Did a doctor and baseball umpire invent safe sex for bachelors and bachelorettes who wanna do the wild thing?" Irish Marvel responds: "No. There's nothing cool, sweet, or *safe* about singles breaking God's sex rule! Besides, *no sex* has ever been listed as the cause of death on anyone's death certificate. In the Bible a.k.a. our life manual, sex outside of a traditional marriage is called fornication. The Scripture at 1 Corinthians 6:18 says to flee from fornication because it's a sin against one's body. Fornication is like a blind person playing with lit dynamite. Still, impatient people take that *long-term* risk for *short-term* happiness. Our planet would actually be a much happier place if people didn't fornicate. There'd be no sexually transmitted cancers or sexually transmitted infections a.k.a. STIs. Unfit, unwed parents who're unprepared for their unwanted children would be a thing of the past."

Teacher shows a male condom and says: "Condoms are a cheap over-the-counter form of contraceptive. They're designed to stop egg and sperm from coming together. Condoms *reduce* the risk of pregnancy and STIs by 98 percent if used correctly. The balloon-looking barrier can slip off. It can get stuck in the vagina and have to be removed by a doctor to prevent infection if trapped more than a few hours. Beware, counterfeiters can make fake condoms. A biking-short style prophylactic hasn't been invented. Condoms don't protect your *entire* genital area. Some STIs are spread through skin-to-skin contact. STIs may also be passed through blood and breast milk. The flimsy elastic doesn't safeguard your reputation, emotions, money, or future. A German study in 2004 found 29 out of 32 condom brands, including all U.S. brands, contain N-nitrosamine, a cancer-causing chemical. A list of the 29 condom brands isn't available to the public because it would hurt the wiener wrapper industry. Ask yourselves: 'Is trusting my life to a breakable piece of rubber that's not 100 percent effective and likely toxic, a *wise* choice?' "

Dr. O'Brien talks about a female condom, holds one up, and says: "We're now going to practice putting on a male condom on a pretend penis." Teacher passes around a basket of condoms. Mr. Windfeather passes around a basket of toy bananas, toy corn dogs, and toy zucchinis. Irish Marvel passes around a basket of scissors. Teacher instructs class on cutting the wrapper, proper condom placement, and explains the rules so learners know not to blow the condoms up or fill them up with water to have a condom scrimmage. When their practice session ends, toys and scissors are collected. Condoms and wrappers are trashed. Group washes their hands.

Irish Marvel warns: "Like the opening bell at the New York Stock Exchange, sex is a bell you can't unring. Some colleges have a zero-tolerance policy for unmarried students having hookups. Before marriage, our private parts function for two reasons only: (1) flush out waste and (2) development from childhood to adulthood. Beware of sneaky folks who *falsely* think there are loopholes around Jehovah's commandment about fornication. Sneaky folks will tell you that it's OK to masturbate a.k.a. have solo sex. That means to rub your private parts for pleasure. They'll also tell you that it's OK to mutually masturbate, meaning two people rub each other's private parts for pleasure. Sneaky folks won't tell you: (A) it's a sexual activity, (B) it's addictive just like vaping, smoking, drugs, and alcohol, plus (C) it's an unclean habit in Jehovah's eyes."

Dr. O'Brien asks: "How many of you have heard of sexting? Webcam models?" Everyone raises a hand. Irish Marvel says: "Sexting *isn't* the norm in a healthy relationship. Sending steamy text messages, underwear shots, or partially or fully nude pictures electronically is bad netiquette. Asking for nudes or sending unwanted nudes is considered sexual harassment. In some states, underage sexts are a crime and senders could face criminal charges. As for webcam models, working as a sexy camgirl or camboy isn't easy money and harmless acting. Sexting and camming are dangerous choices that may forever haunt someone *and* their family. They also open the door for predators to engage in sextortion, revenge porn, kidnapping, human trafficking, torture, and murder."

Valerie asks: "Did you eat googobs of yams or take fertilizer drugs like Octomom?" Dr. O'Brien answers: "I didn't load up on yams or use *fertility* treatments like Nadya Suleman."

B-Raid says: "Lady Luck must've been on your side. Did you cha-ching at a casino on a one-armed bandit with three 4Xs on the payline, scratch off three 4Xs on a scratcher, or eat a boatload of Lucky Charms to get triple lucky?" Dr. O'Brien hums Frank Sinatra's "Luck Be a Lady Tonight" and responds: "No gambling. Nor did I rub a Buddha statue's belly or eat a mother lode of magically delicious cereal. We were blessed to naturally conceive all our fantastic fours. Natural quadruplet odds are 1 in 729,000 births."

Valerie inquires: "Did you and your lucky star go to Lamont classes?" Lucky Star tells: "We didn't participate in those natural childbirth classes because *Lamaze* is designed mostly for parents expecting one child. We chose Marvelous Multiples birth classes."

Betty asks: "Irish Marvel, did you have to poke your cucumber into Dr. O'Brien's cucumber canal four times to become a quad dad?" Cool as a cucumber, he explains: "Every time our reproductive cells got eggcited by playing connect four, one prod with the love rod sealed the deal. Our triad of fraternal quads happened when my wife hyperovulated four eggs, which spontaneously joined with four of my sperm. Each time, it was like four separate pregnancies rolled into one."

Kathy Rose says: "Irish Marvel is as tall as the Jolly Green Giant. You're shorter than Amy Winehouse without her beehive and an inch shorter than Snooki without her poof. So, is there some special way height-challenged couples smush?" Dr. O'Brien tells: "The short and tall of it is that Jehovah invented positions for married couples of all heights and weights."

Fran says: "There's a song that claims sex is healing. Can getting it on heal my grumpy gampy's pancake cancer?" Dr. O'Brien states: "Sorry to hear about his *pancreatic* cancer. I remember meeting Mr. Sheffield during Open House. He reminded me of Andy Rooney because of his bushy, untrimmed eyebrows. I found him to be a tell-it-like-it-is kind of guy. Back to your question, some people call the penis a magic stick, but sex doesn't have any magical powers. 'Sexual Healing' by Marvin Gaye is just a catchy track."

Tiny inquires: "Is it true people can pretend to boink over the phone, on the Net, and even with a blowup doll?" Irish Marvel says: "Yes. People can have phone sex, cybersex, and use a love doll."

Gracie asks: "What do fuzzy handcuffs, leather, chains, blindfolds, a safeword, whip-cracking, and a woman in a catsuit gotta do with sex?" Dr. O'Brien answers: "Some kinky prisoners of love are into role-playing and bondage, meaning they like to be tied up during sex." Kids reply, "Holy cow!"

Dolf tells: "I heard people can get their freak on using their pie holes, keisters, and animals." Irish Marvel says: "Ten-four. Those sex acts are possible 'cause our bods have orifices a.k.a. openings. People can engage in vaginal sex, oral sex, anal sex, and bestiality. FYI: Condoms can get stuck in the pooper." In disgust and disbelief, kids respond, "Nu-uh!" They also make puking gestures and upchucking noises.

Lynn connects the dots and tells Kathy Rose: "That must be how gay people do the oochie coochie. They use their or-stuff." Kathy Rose tells Lynn: "That'd totally explain why my parents sent me to my room when I asked them how gays do the horizontal hula."

Charlotte inquires, "What's a sex toy?" Irish Marvel informs: "It's a device some adults use during sex or as a substitute for sex with a warm body."

Ray Ray asks: "Are sex toys earsplitting like arcade games?" Dr. O'Brien says: "Some of them vibrate like a cellular phone."

Fran inquires: "Is a sex toy and sex object the same thing?" Irish Marvel answers: "No. Sex object means a *person* is used for sex only."

Tiny asks: "So, what does a sex toy look like?" Dr. O'Brien explains: "There are different types of sex toys. The battery-operated ones that resemble male and female sex organs are the most popular. Class, if you ever see something you think could possibly be a sex toy or a condom without the sealed square foil wrapper, don't touch it! It may be contaminated with Donovanosis, the flesh-eating STI that causes privates to decay away."

Mr. Windfeather asks: "Isn't there a vaccine for one of those STIs?" Dr. O'Brien says: "There's a 3-shot Human Papilloma Virus (HPV) vaccine for boys and girls 11 or 12."

Dreadhead inquires: "Can doctors order a virgin test from the two Virginia states, the Virgin Islands, or from that bazillionaire with Virgin businesses everywhere?" Irish Marvel responds: "No. Richard Branson is a tycoon with more than 400 Virgin companies. Just so there's no blurred lines, a virgin is a person who never had any type of sex with another person, device, object, or animal."

Betty asks: "So, how does someone become a born-again virgin?" Irish Marvel says: "It's a made-up term for a single person who was sexually *active* in the past but is sexually *inactive* in the present."

Dr. O'Brien tells: "First-time sex is a soul-joining milestone. Times we're living in, the specialness of sex is so watered down. It isn't unusual for folks to sit around and exchange memories of their first time like they're telling campfire stories."

Irish Marvel says: "Your v-card isn't a give-it-to-someone-and-get-it-out-the-way type of thing. God intended it to be a priceless gift exchange between man and wife. Knowing that, you still may feel it's OK to lose your virginity on prom night or when someone worthy comes along. Blow the whistle right now because that idea simply means you're waiting for the *right* situation to do the *wrong* thing. Therefore, until you're ready to portray the marriage chapter of your life with your leading man or lady, breast and the genital area should remain virgin territories. If you're worried about the virgin/non-virgin scenario, don't be. A non-virgin who loves a virgin won't view the v-card as too much pressure or a turn off."

Dr. O'Brien states: "If you're thinking a doctor could play virgin detective, you're somewhat correct. The doctor could look for clues to disprove a female's virginity such as torn vaginal tissue, semen in the vagina, or obvious signs of STIs. However, a virgin could be born with an STI or get an STI from hair waxing. A female can get pregnant artificially and still be a virgin. Likewise, a male could beget a child artificially and still be a virgin. A doctor can't tell for sure if a female is a virgin or not. Likewise, a doctor can't tell for sure whether a male is a virgin or not. A doctor has to ask the patient to get a definitive answer."

Manners Alert

Attention: Nosey Parkers and Oversharers

Mind Your Own Beeswax!

Irish Marvel tells: "It's unmannerly to ask a single adult if he/she has ever been out on a date, ever been kissed, ever had a girlfriend/boyfriend, or ever been in love. It's also ill-mannered to ask a single adult if he/she dates, is still a virgin, or celibate. Asking about his/her first kiss or seeking deets about losing his/her virginity is bad-mannered. If a single adult *wants* to talk about his/her love life, he/she will *voluntarily* do so."

Dr. O'Brien states: "Sex should always be something two unrelated *grown-ups* agree to do. Forcing a minor or an adult to have any type of sex is a crime. If it happens to you, stand up for yourself whether someone tries to buy your silence with gifts or tries to scare you with threats. Tell a trustworthy adult who'll believe you: your parents, a teacher, doctor, police officer, or 9-1-1 operator. Don't blame yourself or be ashamed. In Jehovah's eyes, a person whose virginity was forcibly taken is still a virgin because it wasn't given by choice."

Floppy asks: "Can astronauts and cosmonauts make whoopee up there in space?" Irish Marvel answers: "In America, space travelers are called *astronauts*. In Russia, they're called *cosmonauts*. Space sex would be challenging. Astronauts and cosmonauts float because of zero gravity. Someone would have to invent a large heavy-duty band to keep the voyagers together."

Kathy Rose inquires: "Could the astronaut say, 'Houston, we have a problem' and ask NASA for some red sex tape?" Dr. O'Brien explains: "Sex tape isn't colored or an adhesive. Some grown-ups like to tape themselves having sex." Students reply, "Ew!"

Irish Marvel says: "Grown-ups refer to skin flicks and other X-rated images as pornography, porno, or porn. Those images can be on TV, electronic devices with Internet access, video games as well as in movies, books, and magazines. Natural curiosity can lure adults and kids to it. Porn is *not* normal. It's unrealistic, disrespectful, addictive, encourages selfishness, destroys marriages, and ruins lives. Porn overloads and rewires the male brain. It can cause healthy males to have a penis performance problem. Porn tricks women into feeling badly about themselves if that smut isn't tolerated. Don't be ensnared … train your brain to say 'no to porno.' "

Stevie tells: "Before summer school ended last year, a new kid on the block invited me to a sleepover. Edna, the au pair, and I heard his grandparents arguing. They were cussing about a little blue pill and what I thought was *corn* on the computer."

Betty says: "I wanna know about a threesie. I figure it got something to do with doing the nasty. One night, after hearing my nudist neighbor's dog howl and a male cricket chirp (female crickets don't chirp), I got up to pee. After making my wish upon a star, I overheard my dad tell my mom that he wanted a threesie. She told him that when she got married she didn't sign up for a throuple or a cavity. My mom lost me with that 'cavity' talk. After that, she smacked his face three times and asked, 'How's that for a threesie?' Next, my mom gave my dad that mama-said-knock-you-out look and punched his lights out. When she cooled off, she apologized, gave him a frozen pack of Potatoes O'Brien for his shiner, and told him that she'd make them an appointment with a marriage counselor. Next day, I wanted to ask her what he meant, but I chickened out." Afterward, Irish Marvel remembers a Vanity 6 song and explains: "A threesie is three-way sex involving three *nasty* people wrapped up in a fantasy world. That 'cavity' talk was about *depravity*. Depravity happens when people lose all sense of right and wrong."

Dr. O'Brien remarks: "Our immoral planet is pretty cray-cray! Obeying God's commandment *not* to hump around is rare and considered old-fashioned. Parenthood is valued above spousehood and marriage gets a bum rap."

Irish Marvel explains: "The Bible tells singles at Colossians 3:5 to *deaden* their body members. If you start dating before you're ready to get married, you'll *awaken* those body members. Girls, ask yourselves: 'Do I really want a guy who thinks, why should I buy the cow when I can get the milk for free?' Boys, ask yourselves: 'Do I really want a gal who thinks, why should I buy the pig when I can get the bacon for free?' Doing right by God and your bod isn't being silly or a negative trait. It doesn't mean you're uncool, you don't want to be loved, or you're an oddball from Virgin, Utah. Nor does it make you undatable, a prude, or future terrorist."

Mr. Windfeather tells: "I've heard of cases in the Dominican Republic and elsewhere that it's possible for girls to grow a penis at 12. The genetic condition is called Guevedoces. It occurs when a boy has the XY chromosome, but private-part wise appears to be a girl at birth. A genetic mishap in the womb stops the male hormone testosterone from changing into another hormone called dihydrotestosterone or DHT for short. Without DHT, the male private parts don't grow properly. Even though the condition is rare, it's a great reason *not* to start dating too early."

Dr. O'Brien says: "Ball's in your court. Take a stance while you think sex is icky. Making and sticking with the right choice about sex that pleases Jehovah won't be easy-peasy. Being responsible for your health, having an achy breaky heart, and trying to heal from the guilt and other consequences because of a wrong choice is much harder. When you attend secondary school, watch out because the *real* losers who're stuck on stupid will scheme and lie to get you to do sexual favors." After that, Irish Marvel remembers an Apollonia 6 song and tells: "There's nothing dirty, bad, or wrong about being a sex shooter as long as you're aiming in your *spouse's* direction. Bottom line: Whether you're in love or not, there's absolutely no benefit whatsoever in knowing someone in the biblical sense before marriage."

Mr. Windfeather asks: "Should my preadolescent great-nieces take an abstinence pledge, wear a promise ring, or attend a purity ball so everyone will know they're not spoiled brats sowing their wild oats?" Irish Marvel answers: "Praying to the Greek goddess Artemis or swimming in the Virgin River won't help, either. Advertising who's aboard the *abstain train* could backfire. There's no guarantee a promise ring will be replaced with a wedding ring."

Fran asks: "If Jordin Sparks or Tim Tebow gets married, do they hafta wear white on their special day?" Dr. O'Brien states: "All nearlyweds, virgins and non-virgins, may wear whatever color they like when they wed."

Lynn inquires: "Do the band or DJ automatically play Madonna's 'Like a Virgin' at the wedding reception if the bride and/or groom is a virgin?" Irish Marvel responds: "Only if it's okay with the newlyweds."

Mary Starlett asks: "Who holds the shotgun at a shotgun wedding?" Dr. O'Brien replies: "Nobody, although many unhappy parents have dreamt about holding one during their child's shotgun wedding. The hurried wedding ceremony happens when a couple is hurled into a shotgun marriage to beat the telltale baby bump because they already did the mattress mambo with each other or the bride-to-be is pregnant by someone other than the groom-to-be. Either way, the couple avoid having the illegitimately conceived kid born out of wedlock and the baby labeled as a fornication byproduct, love child, by-blow, oopsy baby, illegitimate child, or the other swearword that rhymes with mustard."

B-Raid inquires: "At a shotgun reception, do Kathy Bates and James Caan from *Misery* sing a karaoke duet of 'Shotgun'?" Irish Marvel answers: "Nope, but that'd be rib-tickling."

Dr. O'Brien shows a dodecahedron made with her children's faces and says: "Here's a DVD about our 12 progenies." Shortly after the video stops, Valerie comments: "Your Irish terrier, Irish setter, and Irish water spaniel are adorable." Teacher tells: "After the birth of each quad set, in-laws in the UK gifted us a furbaby."

Mary Starlett asks: "Why'd the DVD say something about a calendar marriage?" Irish Marvel explains: "When the *groom* is 11 years older or more, it's called a *May-December* marriage. The younger yokemate is considered to be in the *spring* or early part of life." Dr. O'Brien explains: "When the *bride* is 11 years older or more, it's called a *December-May* marriage. The older yokemate is considered to be in the *winter* or late part of life."

Irish Marvel says: "Some describe an age-gap marriage like ours as gold digging, robbing the cradle, fortune hunting, and bassinet banging. My truelove and I don't trip about any of those negative descriptions. We know our fruitful marriage is genuine."

Yingjie asks: "Is it true people can freeze their eggs and sperm if they're sick or want tots later?" Irish Marvel answers: "Yes. They may be frozen at a hospital or bank inside a clinic for a *chance* at a future baby. Cryopreservation is also available for parents in need of a savior child to save a sick sib."

Rudy inquires: "Before your little ones were born, did everybody know their names?" Dr. O'Brien responds: "We didn't give our blessings fetal monikers. Each kid was the first person to hear the name."

Mr. Windfeather asks: "Did y'all use that gender prediction test? I think it's called IntelliGender." Irish Marvel replies: "Our school of thought regarding gender was it'd be fun to be surprised at the happy event."

Yingjie inquires: "Irish Marvel, did you and your two-in-one ever go on a babymoon?" Basketballer answers: "We didn't know about the pregnancy vacay until we recently went to a gender reveal party. If we're going to be camped out at the maternity ward again, we'll book a babymoon."

B-Raid asks: "Before babies kaboom out the birth cannon, how do baby catchers know the number of babies on board? Do they use a hi-tech airport machine or a crystal ball like that Egyptian TV psychic, Miss Cleopatra?" Dr. O'Brien explains: "An obstetrician, meaning a pregnancy doc, goes by an ultrasound scan. It picks up sound waves from the belly to create a sonogram, which is a computerized baby pic. Every time we were expecting, the sonogram technician pointed out four alien-like wombmates with four heartbeats on a grainy black-and-white screen."

Dreadhead inquires: "Didn't you get tired of peeing on yourself every time your grand-slam babies were coming?" Dr. O'Brien says: "No. The fetus grows in a sac that serves as protection from outside forces. When the fetus is ready to make its debut, the amniotic sac breaks and the amniotic fluid, which is mostly water, is released through the vagina. Each time my water broke, I knew it wasn't pee because the gush was uncontrollable."

Betty asks: "Why do rugrats grow in three semesters?" Dr. O'Brien replies: "*Trimester* means three months. Trimester is how people track the pregnancy timeline and the baby's estimated due date. First trimester is conception, meaning becoming pregnant, to week 14. Second trimester is week 14 to week 28. Third trimester is week 28 to birth. Full-term babies are born between 37 and 42 weeks. Those born after 42 weeks are post-term babies."

Mr. Windfeather comments: "Speaking of pregnancy, I heard it can happen outside the uterus and a fertilized egg can develop into a tumor." Dr. O'Brien responds: "Ectopic pregnancies and molar pregnancies are rare and not viable."

Ponytail inquires: "How long did all your buns bake in your oven?" Dr. O'Brien answers: "My oven's timer beeped at 37 weeks with each high-risk pregnancy. Most four-packs are pre-term a.k.a. preemies born between 29 and 34 weeks of gestation, meaning a baby's growth time in the uterus. Micro preemies are born before 26 weeks or weigh less than 1 pound, 12 ounces at birth."

Dolf comments: "On the telly they always show preemie quads going to the Neonatal Intensive Care Unit for weeks or months. So, I thought quads were like real-life Cabbage Patch preemies." Dr. O'Brien responds: "We were really blessed to have a baby buggy filled with healthy four tops born weighing at least five pounds. None of our neonates had to go to the NICU. Each time, all five of us checked out of the hospital together."

Ray Ray says: "Brian, my potty-mouthed streetballer cousin in juvie, is an only child. He was born butt first. So, everybody calls him 'Butthead.' The kid thinks it's supercool because he did something nobody in the family had done. Did all your children pop out your launch pad head first?" Dr. O'Brien answers: "Yes. Each labor of love had a cephalic presentation, meaning head first. Only 3 percent of quads enter the world vaginally. Sometimes, babies have a breech birth, meaning delivered buttock or feet first. Head first is the safest position because the baby gets enough oxygen and allows room for the rest of the body to be pushed out."

Superboy asks: "Isn't it true that some babies are born with a stork bite or born dead?" Irish Marvel replies: "Most stork bites, which are birthmarks that may appear on the face or neck, usually go away before age three." Dr. O'Brien explains: "A *miscarriage* happens when a baby is spontaneously lifeless at 19 weeks or less. If a baby is spontaneously lifeless after 20 weeks, the baby is considered *stillborn*."

Mr. Windfeather says: "Class should know that not every married couple want to bring up children. It's OK to be a nuclear dyad family, meaning a married *childfree* couple, as long as both agree. There's nothing in the wedding vows that says childrearing is a requirement for a long and happy marriage." Dr. O'Brien responds, "Thanks for mentioning that."

Irish Marvel says: "You-all may be wondering what happened to my wife's smaller stunners." Students nod "yes." Dr. O'Brien informs: "We didn't sell them on eBay, advertise them for sale on Craigslist, hock them at a pawn shop, or lose them playing poker. I kept my first bridal set … engagement ring and wedding band. The other two upgraded rings were sold at a bazaar for our foundation."

Shakobe inquires: "Did y'all have a kissing booth like they had on my favorite episode of *The Wayans Bros.* when they went to a church bazaar?" Irish Marvel answers: "Nope. When a man swaps saliva a.k.a. swap spit with a woman while playing the kissing game, he slips her testosterone. In turn, the male hormone testosterone causes a lady to have lovey-dovey feelings for a guy." Next, group listens to Betty Everett's "The Shoop Shoop Song (It's in His Kiss)."

Dr. O'Brien informs: "As a golden rule, we're only allowed to kiss each other on the soup coolers. Our lips are banned from kissing our kids, close relatives, comrades, and pets on the mouth. Both of us are germaphobes. So, the thought of secondhand kissing other people, catching a cold, getting hepatitis B, warts, cavities, gum disease, herpes infection, the flu, infectious mononucleosis a.k.a. kissing disease, or meningococcal disease totally squashed that idea. Researchers say that a first-time smooch is more powerful than first-time sex. In fact, some couples save the first kiss for their wedding day." Mary Starlett asks, "Are they nutty cult people?" Irish Marvel responds: "No. It's a choice some couples feel is right for them."

Teacher states: "No more suspense. Time to yield up. First, I need a drum roll." Irish Marvel pulls out a set of Djembe African drums out of the teacher's closet and plays them for 22 seconds. Dr. O'Brien reveals: "My ring secret is … it has a hidden monitor. When I flip up the sapphire in the center where the monitor is, I can see and speak with my immediate family. It also has live pro basketball access. My ring is inscribed with the inscription: You Got the Best of My Love. It's waterproof and has a glittery strobe light that glows in the dark."

Dolf says: "Your ice, ice baby is more fabulous than Princess Diana's engagement ring. Are you scurred someone will steal your big ole ice?" Dr. O'Brien answers: "No. My regal ring is equipped with state-of-the-art security features. First alarm has a red rotating light with a wailing siren like a fire truck. After the siren stops, Beyoncé's signature song, 'Single Ladies (Put a Ring on It)' plays." Next, teacher pushes a button to activate the alarm and does a jaw-dropping Beyoncé impression so incredible, Beyoncé's alter-ego, Sasha Fierce, would be jealous. When the chorus comes, everyone sings, "Woo oh ooh oh oh ooh oh oh ooh oh oh oh!"

Dr. O'Brien informs: "Second alarm plays the instrumental intro to Anita Ward's 'Ring My Bell' and sends a silent ding-dong to the nearest police station. Third alarm plays the chorus to Mario's 'Let Me Love You.' After Mario sings his lyrics, 'Baby good love and protection,' I make my selection … stun gun if the crook is close enough to zap or the Taser if he/she isn't more than 15 feet away. Fourth alarm features a teakettle-sounding whistle that rises to 133 decibels. It also releases steam scented with a stinky skunk spray that stings. The fifth alarm is booby-trapped with a pomegranate juice dye pack. Sixth alarm plays a musical rotation only the po-po can disable. A remix of Con Funk Shun's 'Chase Me' plays followed by a remix of Rockwell's 'Somebody's Watching Me.' Whichever alarm I choose, I can always trigger the discharge of Silly String. My ring also has a tracking device and HD webcam so a jewel thief like 79-year-old Doris Payne can't quote Shaggy by claiming, "It wasn't me."

Ray Ray asks: "How's it possible for all your good-haired, preppy kids to see and talk with you?" Dr. O'Brien answers: "Our privileged descendants wear bracelets with a hidden monitor that Mr. Windfeather custom-made for them."

Stevie says: "You're a first-class basketball wife with mother wit. Would you ever have your own reality TV show or join the catfighting cast of *Basketball Wives*?" Dr. O'Brien responds: "We're not a chippy couple. Irish Marvel and I know what true love is. We advocate family values. So, probably not. We don't want to be a supercouple whose lives are a train wreck and see the aftermath on somebody's blog or TMZ. However, I wouldn't mind a guest appearance or recurring role on *Army Wives, The Good Wife,* or *Desperate Housewives.*"

Mary Starlett says: "You two are a cute ice-cream castle couple who won't be on *I Didn't Know I Was Pregnant* or *Jerry Springer* acting a darn fool. Your marriage survived longer than John and Kate Gosselin's. We won't see y'all on *Maury* or *Divorce Court* telling all your Kool-Aid, explaining baby mama/baby daddy drama, waiting for a DNA result, being hooked up to a lie-detector machine, or embarrassing yourselves behind some marriage mess. We won't hear about y'all embroiled in a custody battle like the parents in that *What Color Is Love?* Lifetime movie. People can't say that Irish Marvel is a deadbeat dad or Dr. O'Brien is a deadbeat mom. You two keepers are doting parents, kindred spirits, a class act, and have a rock-solid marriage. Now, 'Solid' by Ashford & Simpson is playing in my head. We can tell by how well you treat each other in private and in public. Y'all are a ballerific ebony-and-ivory version of Demi Moore and Ashton Kutcher, except Demi has been to the chapel of love three times."

Mr. Windfeather says: "I know if y'all call it quits and have a co-parenting relationship, Dr. O'Brien won't pick and roll with a rebound guy or get tipsy and call 9-1-1 looking for a husband like that lonesome 57-year-old lady on the news. I really hope you two don't pull a 40-year splitter shocker like that power couple, Al and Tipper Gore, because y'all grew apart."

Dr. O'Brien states: "We're not a childish cop-out couple. A truly committed couple don't take a timeout, breakup, or have an on-again, off-again relationship. They do the teamwork to make a marriage last until death do them part. The ultimate union isn't just lip service and a piece of paper. It's an institution and a covenant." Kids reply, "What's a covenant?" Irish Marvel explains: "Regarding marriage, covenant is a lifelong agreement couples make before God to live up to their vows."

Mr. Windfeather comments: "I know Irish Marvel doesn't wanna get up early in the morning to find him another lover like that Gap Band song says." Irish Marvel responds: "I would be lovesick, fosheezy! I'm no early bird. Even if I burned rubber, the worm would be long gone. Yours truly is a night owl."

Dr. O'Brien says: "We're not a garden-variety couple. I'm from the Baby Boomer Generation (born 1946-1964). My mate is from Generation X (born 1965-1980). We took the plunge when I was 45 and my swain was 22. Our love story was highlighted during the wedding ceremony. In honor of our 23-year age difference, we jumped over the broom after guests counted aloud 23 seconds into the intro of 'Jump (for My Love)' by the Pointer Sisters."

Mr. Windfeather states: "Mamma mia! You and youngblood completely defied that half-your-age-plus-seven date rule. Do either one of you think your ancestors would be disappointed or feel betrayed because you didn't marry one of your own?" Irish Marvel replies, "I doubt it." Dr. O'Brien says: "Given my age in *today's* world, I think they'd give me mad props for bravely stepping outside the box and say that my patience paid off big-time." Yingjie jokes: "I think they'd be cool with it once they heard we've been living as one nation under a groove since 1978."

Fran asks: "At the bridal shop, did a saleslady hear your age and think you were shopping as a groom mom, or for your daughter's wedding dress?" Dr. O'Brien responds: "Nope, but I'd be lying through my teeth if I said those thoughts never crossed my mind. One wedding vendor overheard I'm middle-aged and told his Millennial intern that I should focus *less* on *wedding* planning and focus *more* on *will* planning." Mr. Windfeather asks: "Was he being pessimistic or realistic?" Teacher replies, "Honestly, both."

Irish Marvel says: "The object of my affection is the oldest lady in the history of professional basketball to join the first wives club. When we first became an item, shade-throwers saw us as the laughingstock of the league. Fast-forward to now, we're having the last laugh. Those same shade-throwers had a change of heart. They see us a role-model couple and beg us for relationship advice."

Shakobe asks: "Any wedding woes? Did something unusual go down at y'alls big event like a magician turned water into wine?" Irish Marvel answers: "Let me think. A jilted old flame didn't fan the flames by requesting Vesta's awkward 'Congratulations' song on the radio. Neither of us had pre-wedding jitters or got cold feet. I didn't call off the wedding on our wedding day. When we got spliced, my bride had every bridal token: something old, something new, something borrowed, something blue, and a silver sixpence in her left shoe. We didn't use a decoy bride. Armed bodyguards didn't pose as undercover groomsmen or bridesmaids. Nobody objected. Etta James didn't sing 'Stop the Wedding.' There were no crazed fans, hecklers, gatecrashers, stalkers, flashers, gropers, or guests gone wild who got plastered and landed in the drunk tank. Watching CNN the next day, we heard Wolf Blitzer from *The Situation Room* report a helicopter circled Neverland until it ran out of gas. The pilot and her paparazzi passenger landed in the middle of MJ's black mamba snake den. Animal trainers rescued the unharmed partners in crime and they were arrested for trespassing. All in all, we got hitched without a hitch."

Dreadhead inquires: "Speaking of reptiles, is it true Ireland doesn't have snakes?" Dr. O'Brien says: "By show of hands, how many thinks it's true?" Students are split fifty-fifty. Irish Marvel answers: "Those cold-blooded animals were never there. They couldn't hiss or slither their way through the ice ages. Today, snakes are used as pets and zoo attractions in the Land of Saints and Scholars."

Dr. O'Brien states: "Back to Shakobe's question, it wasn't about a David Blaine illusion or a Kazaam genie wish being granted. Jesus performed his first *miracle* at a marriage feast in Cana when the wine ran low. Our only Jesus-juice action was that someone requested DJ Heavy D to play UB40's 'Red Red Wine' at the reception."

Tiny asks: "Did y'all go on a second honeymoon for your 10-year anniversary?" Irish Marvel says: "We had a still do soirée. Judge Ephriam and Judge Wapner spoke some words of wisdom. After amusingly saying our 'I still do's' to married life, Shania Twain sang an a cappella version of 'You're Still the One I Love' and New Edition sang 'I'm Still in Love with You.'"

Superboy has an aha moment and says: "True love may be hard to find, but it has nothing to do with stupid stuff like age, color, height, weight, or education." Irish Marvel states: "You hit the nail on the head! We have true grit. None of that *Shallow Hal* baloney was a deal breaker for us. That's why I always bring my wife a dozen blue roses. They suggest something unachievable. We didn't wait on the world to change like that song by John Mayer. Instead, we took Bonnie Raitt's advice and gave people something to talk about. A rumor mill wrongly accused my intended of being a man-eating, jersey chaser looking for a meal ticket. Some said that I was looking for a mother figure. Others assumed our unusual pairing was about bragging rights. Most considered our trip down the aisle a misstep and a recipe for disaster – not compatible and nothing in common. Skeptics alleged our marriage was a bigger stunt than Balloon Boy trapped inside a flying saucer. Scores of Internet trolls thought we were crazy as H-E-double-hockey-sticks! Critics called us 'the odd couple' and tagged our linkup as a starter marriage. A few reduced it to a tax-credit marriage. Many years ago, we sued and won $4.8 million because a trash-talking tabloid lied about us having a green-card marriage."

Mr. Windfeather comments: "Anyone thinking your marriage is a mistake or fake is mistaken. It's evident you two complement one another and want the same things in life."

Floppy tells Yingjie: "My aunt and uncle in Kansas City went from *just friends* to *just married* in three weeks. I heard it's a bogus g-card marriage. My mom's kid sister and her out-of-work husband have six little rascals. When those two aren't fighting, they are always complaining about the same old stuff: the pump jump, all of their bills, the economy, and living paycheck-to-paycheck off one income." Yingjie tells Floppy: "Sounds like a *real* marriage to me."

Dr. O'Brien says: "The most hurtful potshot of all was being branded a spinster sperm-jacker." Mr. Windfeather asks: "Is that an unattached dame over 35 suffering from FOMO who sticks up a sperm bank?" Irish Marvel answers: "It's a fertile, never-married woman past her prime who's panicky 'cause she's childless. So, the broody lady goes on the prowl seeking an unsuspecting, ideal young buck in hopes of attaining the crown jewel – a baby."

Ponytail inquires: "If the fountain of youth isn't discovered soon, are you afraid your b-baller hubster will trade you for a P.Y.T.?" Young-at-heart basketball wife laughs and confidently replies: "Absolutely not! We have a verbal no-trade clause. Some pretty young thing can't hold a candle to me. I'm also unfazed by meanies who mom-shame me for exercising my prerogative to be an older mother."

Irish Marvel says: "My girl is *wife* enough and *mom* enough not to let our situation freak her out. It just freaks out *judgmental* people. We're used to the I-don't-get-it stare, that what-do-they-see-in-each-other gaze, and the occasional side-eye. One Irish proverb says: 'The older the fiddle, the sweeter the tune.' Sticking to my wife is a no-brainer. I would be an absolute idiot to tank our team and trade the model that's in mint condition and has exceeded my expectations. When it comes to love, it's not about the person's *age*, it's about what's on the person's *page*."

Dr. O'Brien tells: "The Bible says at Proverbs 16:31 that gray-headedness is a crown of beauty if a person lives a righteous life. If my golden years and twilight years are spent as a gray-haired or white-haired woman, I'll embrace it. I plan to age gracefully like Sophia Loren, but I keep Joan River's plastic surgeon's number on speed dial. Besides, I'll stay forever young because I shop at Forever 21."

Charlotte asks: "Do people think your big brood are grandkids or you're the help?" Dr. O'Brien answers: "Most presume our quiverful are grandchildren or I'm a super-young great-grandmother. Others think I'm the housekeeper, governess, or some type of sitter. Many have mistaken my helpmate as an escort, handyman, or manny."

Mr. Windfeather inquires: "Any growing pains, sibling rivalry, bad-to-the-bone bebe kids, or signs of silver spoon syndrome?" Together tough-love parents say: "No … not yet … none at all … and hopefully never."

Stevie asks: "Irish Marvel, aren't you sad you can't see and talk with your Big 12?" Basketballer says: "Nope. I have a secret to reveal. First, I will need a drum roll." Dr. O'Brien plays the Djembe African drums for 22 seconds. Pointing at his watch that's encrusted with diamonds and emeralds, Irish Marvel reveals: "It has the identical hidden monitor. Wonderful One surprised me after our last baby boom. The inscription reads: I'll Love You Until the End of Time. When I flip up the face, where the monitor is, I can see and speak with my family anytime. I can also catch pro basketball games. My waterproof gift has the same glittery strobe light that glows in the dark."

B-Raid asks: "Does his iced-out timepiece weigh more than her iced-out ring?" Irish Marvel removes his wristwatch and gives it to Mr. Windfeather. The jeweler puts the timekeeper on the jewelry scale and says: "His dazzling diamonds plus the luminous emeralds weigh 10,000 carats just like her 10,000-carat ring."

Dolf inquires: "Could you have gotten a shot, slapped on a patch, taken some horse pills, or gotten hoovered if you only wanted a twofer rather than four peas in a pod?" Dr. O'Brien explains: "The shot, patch, and pills are contraceptives made from synthetic hormones to prevent pregnancies. They don't *control* the number of births. There's no family planning a.k.a. birth control option that's 100 percent effective. Hoovered is slang for abortion. It's an operation that ends a pregnancy. It can cause a heap of health problems, lead to certain cancers, and possibly death. Doctors can also do candy-coated, abortion-like procedures such as selective reduction and gender selection. Still, the outcome is a cupcake kid, meaning an unborn child *intentionally* denied a birthday."

Yingjie tells: "I heard that it's okay to get scraped at the abortuary if somebody attacked the mom, or the mom did the deed with a family member, or the doc thinks the mom and/or the baby won't make it." Dr. O'Brien shows abortion photos from the Net and responds: "People who're pro-*life* feel abortion is wrong. People who're pro-*choice* feel abortion should be up to the mum. The Bible doesn't make any exceptions for rape, incest, or survival. Sometimes, doing the right thing can result in loss of life."

Ponytail states: "I know those *chemic* baby blockers have side effects. So, can you buy *organic* ones at Whole Foods, Trader Joe's, or Fresh & Easy?" Dr. O'Brien answers, "No can do, kiddo."

Lynn asks: "Is it true the Pill can make ladies pick Mr. Wrong?" Irish Marvel draws a tick in the air with his index finger and says: "Check mark. Females are born with a natural ability to mate with males who have *opposite* body odor. The scent is like a mating call. It's important because it proves a genetic mating match. The smell keeps Mr. Right and Ms. Right attracted to one another. The Pill completely throws off a fertile female's sense of smell."

Mr. Windfeather inquires: "So, what's the difference between the Pill and that touted morning-after pill?" Dr. O'Brien explains: "The Pill is prescribed and taken every day. The morning-after pill is considered emergency contraception. It's one drugstore pill taken within 72 hours after sex to prevent pregnancy."

Fran tells: "Last month, my aunt Farrah told my nana that she was caught between her sugar daddy and secret lover in some psycho love triangle. Three weeks later, Aunt Farrah finally admitted she's in the pudding club. When Nana heard the preggo news, she whacked Aunt Farrah's face and asked her boomerang kid how could she let the rabbit die without having a husband. Dr. O'Brien, you had 12 babies. Were you sad 12 rabbits croaked?" Mr. Windfeather asks: "Would you mind if I explain the saying, 'The rabbit died'?" Teacher answers, "Go ahead, school us."

Mr. Windfeather informs: "According to Wikipedia, there were two male German gynecologists who used mice to invent a pregnancy test in 1927. The doctors who specialized in women's health, injected female rabbits with women's urine. They waited a few days to check the rabbits' ovaries to see if there was a change due to the hormone HCG. People thought all the test rabbits died when the women became pregnant. In actuality, all the test rabbits died because it was costly and troublesome to care for them after the test surgery."

Gracie says: "Yesterday, I overheard my matka and her loud, wine-drinking homegirls talking about a *Sex and the City* episode. They were also complaining about manthers and their dry spells and saying that it's unfair that horny guys in different countries can have more than one wife. Is there someplace where ladies have lotsa husbands?" Dr. O'Brien answers: "Your mother is talking about *polygamy* where men have many wives. On the other hand, *polyandry* is where women have many husbands." Irish Marvel surfs the Web on his smartphone and reports: "According to Wikipedia, polyandry is rare. It's been practiced in the Pacific Islands, Africa, India, Asia, South America, and Europe. Multiple spouses may be acceptable in some places, but it's still wrong."

Rebecca asks: "Speaking of Africa, is it true that little girls in Nigeria get part of their vulvas cut off before they're five?" Dr. O'Brien responds: "Not all, but many have. Female genital mutilation is a devastating *cultural* practice." Rebecca asks: "So, when Jewish baby boys get part of their penis skin cut off, isn't that mutilation, too?" Teacher replies: "Some Jewish parents feel that way about circumcision and respectfully decline that *religious* practice."

Rudy says: "My bad. I meant to ask about your monitors earlier when you two spilled the beans. Do people disappear from both screens when they go potty?" Irish Marvel explains: "We didn't want to be mistaken for perverts. So, we installed a privacy feature. On our monitors, a door appears and a message reads: Please check back later. The person you want to contact is at the lavatory. Would you like to dispatch an e-hug or e-mwah while you wait? If so, press yes to continue."

Betty says: "My sneakerhead cousin, Lela, was sweet on a shooting guard who spoke all five Romance languages. He wasn't top dog like Irish Marvel. Lela's Latin lover was a jersey-popping sixth man on an underdog team below .500. She says that pro basketball players are low-class, immature, too big for their britches, commitment-phobic, braggadocios showoffs, weed-smoking, tattoo junkies, narcissistic, mama's boys, crybabies, strip club goers, materialistic, high-stakes gamblers, video-game playing, orange ball chasers! She also says that they suck at being in a relationship and are either baby-sprinkling jerks or tomcats who step out of bounds on their WAGs. Are you worried the *National Enquirer* will catch your hunky hubby creeping with a scuzzy cheerleader, a trampy video girl, or many skanky jump-offs like they did with that transgressing golfer who shoved his pretty wife into the hurt locker because he didn't keep his tiger in the woods?" True-blue family woman responds: "Nope. Two-timing is a big no-no like a Flagrant 2 foul in basketball. The love of my life doesn't want to be ejected and become a *divorcé* because of a one-night stand or having a *mistress*."

True-blue family man comments: "The love of my life doesn't want to get ejected and become a *divorcée* because of a one-night stand or having a *histress*. Mates with moral compasses, who truly cherish their spouses and treasure their marriages, don't commit adultery by having sex with home-wrecking interlopers such as swingers, prostitutes, gigolos, porn stars, or everyday people. They know there's no amount of pleasure or excitement that outweighs the humiliation and pain the hanky-panky causes the innocent mate and their kids. Some professional ball cads are notorious baby sprinklers and aren't marriage minded or marriage material. It's no secret that many pro sport players have bad track records with women. Nor is it a secret that infidelity in the league is quite common. However, Betty's cousin's characterization of professional basketball players is a stereotype like all Asians are brainiacs. My wife and I have a strong frontcourt and backcourt. It would be ironic for us to juggle a side piece considering our remindful ringtone for each other is 'Bring It on Home to Me' by Sam Cooke."

Rudy inquires: "Speaking of league, did either one of you ever feel like you were out of each other's?" In unison, dream team replies, "Not even for a nanosecond." Dr. O'Brien comments: "Green-eyed monsters told *me* that I was out of *his* and green-eyed monsters told *him* that he was out of *mine*. As long as a person feels good about himself or herself, nobody is out of anybody's league."

Mr. Windfeather asks: "Is it true that men in their 90s can still sire?" Irish Marvel answers: "Yes siree! Although Mother Nature and Father Time aren't real people, they make us think about the aging process. Men's testosterone levels take a tumble after age 30. However, healthy males with quality sperm are able to fecundate well into their golden years. World's oldest papa was 92 when his ninth nenê was born. FYI: Doctors can retrieve sperm up to 36 hours after death."

Dreadhead inquires: "So, how many awesome foursomes can one female have?" Dr. O'Brien replies: "No limit on quadruplicating. Four is the record thus far."

Mr. Windfeather says: "Dr. O'Brien, you truly give new meaning to the Commodores' 'Three Times a Lady.' Were you surprised to have four of a kind thrice?" Teacher says: "I'm *still* surprised. Some days, I have to pinch myself to make sure I'm not dreaming."

Mary Starlett says: "I want y'all to kiss and tell us if Dr. O'Brien can procreate more Black-Rish combo kids or has her biology clock ticked its last tock?" Couple air-kiss, next teacher explains: "Age 25 is ideal. Dr. Oz says that women should have kids before 30 because after that there's an 88 percent drop in the egg supply. As I said that, I thought about Humpty Dumpty and his great fall. Getting back on track, healthy females with quality eggs can bear fruit from puberty until menopause. My *biological* clock is winding down like a 24-second shot clock and ticking louder than Flavor Flav's clock necklace. However, I haven't experienced menopause a.k.a. the change of life, when all my eggcellent bench players are gone and Aunt Flow stopped visiting for 12 consecutive months. Menopause usually happens somewhere between ages 45 and 55. I still have a uterus and I haven't had a bilateral oophorectomy, meaning an operation to remove both ovaries. Therefore, until a baby shot-blocker happens; ladies like me still got a window of opportunity to naturally download bouncing babies."

Mr. Windfeather comments: "Having a full house with a dozen kids, I can't help but wonder if you ever had the baby blues or postpartum depression." Dr. O'Brien replies: "No. Irish Marvel and I were blessed to be at a good place in our lives after each pregnancy, which greatly reduced *both* our chances of experiencing either one."

Jeweler briefly thinks about the term *half-breed* and how it has been used in Native-American history, and then he inquires: "Do people refer to your young'uns as pandas or zebras?" Irish Marvel says: "Sometimes. Our close-knit clan use it as a teachable moment to educate people that Jehovah creates each panda and zebra with a distinctive marking for identification. Their individual black-and-white markings also help both warm-blooded mammals to survive in the wilderness." Dr. O'Brien adds: "We're raising our biracial children to be bicultural. Our kids know that if someone refuses to accept them for who they are or makes them feel like they have to pick a side just to fit in, they should take their friendship and/or business elsewhere."

Tiny remarks: "I hope Dr. O'Brien gets baby fever so her Liberace-ish ring can get even *more* gigantic." Teacher replies: "No more babies on the brain. I'm not a bumpaholic. We don't want our kid count to equal or exceed the Duggar's 19. Doing the baby dance a.k.a. trying to conceive again is highly unlikely, but not impossible. We've joshed about broadening our baby factory to a baker's dozen by adoption or adding a new member via a singleton, meaning baby watch for one sprog."

Rudy asks: "Isn't it bad luck to have 13 niños?" Irish Marvel answers: "Not true. We don't have triskaidekaphobia, which is a fear of the prime number 13."

Dr. O'Brien tells: "We've considered matching a pro team roster of 15 by having triplets or twins plus a singleton. We joked about shooting for a four-point play by quadruplicating again. Since winning the Triple Crown by birthing a senior, junior, and sophomore quad set, our rising stars are hoping for a long shot that I'll have another. Our Pac-12 thinks a freshman fab four would be neato."

Mr. Windfeather comments: "If those two add a singleton, twins, or another set of higher-order multiples to their family troop, I'll gladly make Soldier of Love a larger pushing present and throw in a jumbo toe ring to match. I'm elated it won't be for the married millionaire's mistake." Kids reply, "What's that?" Jeweler tells: "When a rich *unchaste* husband betrays his rich *chaste* wife, he buys her a mansion in the form of a humongous let's-kiss-and-make-up ring. He'd rather do that than wear the scarlet letter A – an embarrassing badge of public shame for being an adulterer. In some cases, also having an adulterine child."

Children talk among themselves while their teacher converses with her mentor, the state superintendent. Afterward, Mr. Windfeather thinks about his kids when they were fifth graders and remarks: "Your sex education program is all-inclusive. I thought students just separately watched a humdrum documentary about the facts-of-life with the school nurse."

Dr. O'Brien tells: "Staff and parents agreed that to be forewarned is to be forearmed especially when it comes to pedophiles." All but one student replies, "What's that?" Betty mouths, "The Pied Piper." Irish Marvel answers: "They're mentally ill people who want to have sex with children or commit the crime of having sex with kids."

Teacher discards last month's newsletter and further explains: "Nurse Núñez, our school nurse, won the $65 million Powerball in May. Day after he cashed his overnight express check, he bounced. Principal Worm decided it'd be more interesting and realistic for *my* class to learn about the birds and the bees collectively from parents of back-to-back-to-back quads. We knew *this* lesson would be the most impactive. Instead of grumbling, we chose to welcome the skills challenge."

Mr. Windfeather states: "Before I met the O'Briens, my ignorant marriage bracket predicted that Magic and Cookie Johnson was the only pro basketball couple that would stay married because Magic is HIV positive. Kudos for proving me wrong."

Sheet Cake comments: "I thought getting married was for bougie White people."

Kathy Rose tells: "Before today, I believed being pronounced husband and wife was unnecessary and obsolete like eight-tracks, telegrams, encyclopedia sets, my uncle Scootie's manual typewriter, and an old-school bachelor's little black book. Now, I know that marriage is a badge of honor for opposite-sex grown-ups who want an everlasting pledge partner to grow old with plus those who want to make and raise a family the right way."

Irish Marvel announces: "In July, we're sending the class to my fun-filled, weeklong basketball camp in Maui." Students shout, "Hoop, hoop hooray!" Dr. O'Brien responds: "During the off-season, when we're not visiting Ireland and Nigeria, Hawaii is home base."

Irish Marvel says: "Joel Osteen will open the summer camp with something funny. Some minor-leaguers, various current and throwback pro players as well as the Harlem Globetrotters will attend. Barry O'Bomber will also attend." Dr. O'Brien cranks up Bruce Springsteen's "Born in the U.S.A." and tells: "In an e-mail, we assured Mr. 44 there'd be no racist monkey business about his birth certificate."

Mr. Windfeather inquires, "Do y'all know Michelle Obama, too?" Dr. O'Brien tells: "In 2001, while vacationing in Chicago, we met our current FLOTUS and POTUS at a couples cooking class."

Irish Marvel reveals: "In September, I'll be packing my athleticism, swiveling hips, and fancy footwork to vie for the mirror ball trophy on *Dancing with the Stars*."

Dr. O'Brien announces: "Irish Marvel and I will run on with Oprah in November to promote the long-awaited birth of my brainchild – a must-read page-turner called *The Ring Secret*. After the show, Gayle and Stedman will join the three of us for lunch."

Mr. Windfeather asks: "What inspired you to pen a Great American Novel or want to become the next J.K. Rowling?" Authoress explains her literary foray: "After eating Chinese food one night, I opened a fortune cookie and the message said: 'You have a charming way with words and should write a book.' Therefore, to see if it was *right*, I had to *write*."

Dr. O'Brien briefly plays the instrumental version of "Save the Best for Last" by Vanessa Williams. Kids recognize the tune and wonder what's next. B-Raid asks: "Does that teaser music mean something amazeballs is coming?" Big3 trio answers, "Absolutely!" Mr. Windfeather adds: "The moment you-all have waited for since late January is finally here. Before the big reveal, I'll need a drum roll from the dynamic duo." Couple play the Djembe African drums for 22 seconds.

Mr. Windfeather says: "Without further ado, we're replacing your artificial rings with the real McCoy. The instrumental music was to tip-off our ring ceremony. Boys are getting a blue box. Girls are getting a pink box. I got everybody's size from that fingerprint project. Everyone is being bestowed with a superb class ring that has your birthstone, school name, current year, and full name engraved. All 22 of you MVPs have attended this distinguished school since kindergarten. The connubial collaborators wanted you-all to have a special memento to remember your grammar school days."

Irish Marvel inquires: "Should I play the song 'Jump' by Van Halen or 'Jump' by Kris Kross for a battle-of-the-sexes jump ball to decide which gender gets their rings first?" Dr. O'Brien answers: "Seeing who controls the tap isn't necessary. We'll go in alphabetical order."

Dr. O'Brien announces: "Time for the icing on the cake. Every fifth grader attending this grade school is receiving a $5,000 donation to his/her college fund courtesy of Irish Marvel and me." After the bighearted announcement, students quote Madea, "Hallelujer!" Afterward, the surprised class has a tearful farewell group hug. Next, the three musketeers stand arm in arm at the front of the classroom as teacher states: "We'll ring down the curtain on our last hurrah with a suitable tribute to the trailblazing conductor, Mr. Don Cornelius. You can bet your last money, it's all gonna be a stone gas, honey! I'm Dr. O'Brien. In parting, we wish you love, peace, and sooouuul!"

Seconds later, dismissal bell rings. Dr. O'Brien flashes her pearly whites and declares, "Class dismissed."

You've reached the end of the fourth quarter. Before you begin the extra frame, listen to "Save the Overtime (For Me)" by Gladys Knight & the Pips.

End of Regulation

Chapter Five

Overtime

Ball

In October 2010, Irish Marvel has a dream during a thunderstorm. He dreams he's having a vasectomy, meaning surgery to stop sperm flow. Same night, his wife has a dream. She dreams she's having a tubal ligation a.k.a. tubes tied. The operation stops the fallopian tubes from allowing an egg to travel to the uterus.

Next morning, the couple awaken from their beauty sleep to Christopher Williams'
"I'm Dreamin' " song on the radio. They laugh as they tell each other about their
dreams. Same afternoon, Dr. O'Brien learns she's with child and is three weeks
along. That evening, the I-thought-I-was-fast-approaching-menopause wife shares
the news with her I-thought-she-was-fast-approaching-menopause husband by
drawing a pair of baby booties on an old Etch A Sketch. The two canoodle and
Irish Marvel quips, "We got an extra credit assignment."

Nine months later, the couple are expecting twins. A last-minute ultrasound reveals two bonus babies playing peek-a-boo and pat-a-cake behind each twin. Planning for the completion of their Big Ten, dumbfounded parents (Dr. O'Brien, 56, and Irish Marvel, 33) react to the four-to-the-second-power update with a Lawler-ism, "Oh me, oh my!" Thirty minutes thereafter, the pair welcome their acquisition via C-section on Independence Day to the sounds of K.P. singing "Firework" and multiple firecrackers exploding at an adjacent park. Sticking with a medal theme, newest sibship is nicknamed "The Pewter Set." Six weeks after the fourpeat, basketballer changes his uniform number to 44.

One month later, TLC airs a primetime edition of *Make Room for Multiples*. First hour highlights a room addition, funny babymoon in Cancún, introduction of the fourth member of the couple's canine family (Irish wolfhound named Wolfgang), a lullaby lip sync battle between Will Ferrell and The Rock plus investment tips from Warren G and Warren Buffett. It concludes with the couple getting sideswiped in a hit-and-run accident during a foggy police pursuit leading to the capture of a Columbian crime boss.

Second hour features a co-ed baby shower designed by Martha Stewart. It includes interviews with an AARP representative, a doula, Supernanny, hospital staff, dignitaries, commissioner and deputy commissioner of pro basketball plus a host of family and friends. Next, there's well-wishes from The Little Couple, Babyface, Adam Sandler, Ruby Dee, Bob Eubanks, Jayne Kennedy, Bono, Robin Roberts, Pat Sajak and Vanna White, Pelé, The Village People, Miley Cyrus, B.B. King accompanied by Lucille, Amy Dickinson, Miguel, Joan Collins, Misty Copeland, Lizzie Velásquez, Arsenio Hall, Casey Kasem, John Travolta, Guillermo, Sinbad, Christiane Amanpour, Lisa Leslie, Vin Scully, Donnie Simpson, Fabio, Ellen, Juwanna Mann, Tom Brady, Nicki Minaj, Larry King, Eve, Jim Hill, Steve Jobs, Percy Sledge, Ole Skool Crew, Psy, Marlee Matlin, Russell Brand, Jackie Chan, Mr. Spock, Floyd Mayweather, Bob Baffert, Mork from Ork, Manny Pacquiao, Cher, Jay Leno, Wonder Woman, David Letterman, Kevin Hart, George Clooney, Brittney Griner, Betty White, R2-D2, *PTI* guys, Morris Day, Richard Simmons, Little Richard, Conor McGregor, Lorena Bobbitt, Kermit, Miss Piggy, Big Bird, Conan O'Brien, Stephen Hawking, and Honey Boo Boo.

After that, Lil Wayne dedicates "How to Love" to Dr. O'Brien because she's really far from the usual. Mick Jagger and The Jacksons sing "State of Shock." Song is appropriate as it echoes how the thunderstruck couple felt when they heard their family was growing four-ward again. Two-hour program culminates with quad's nativity along with Willie Nelson and Waylon Jennings' interactive duet of "Mammas Don't Let Your Babies Grow Up to Be Cowboys."

Before his unexpected dirt nap, Mr. Windfeather made Dr. O'Brien a 12,500-carat wedding ring and matching toe ring. Both eye-popping statement pieces are bejeweled with a heart-shaped sapphire in the center, 12 diamonds, and 4 rubies.

After an active-shooting drill in May of the 2016-2017 academic year, the two inform the fifth-grade class that they'll be the first interracial married couple on the cover of *Ebony* magazine. After that, Irish Marvel explains their good tidings: "The June 2017 issue marks the 50th anniversary of the landmark court case, *Loving v. Virginia*. After Mildred and Richard Loving's nine-year legal battle, the Supreme Court of the United States ruled on Monday, June 12, 1967, that Whites could marry nonwhites in all states. FYI: The building has a basketball court nicknamed 'Highest Court in the Land' on the fifth floor."

In mid-July 2017, one month after Irish Marvel wins his seventh championship (Game 7 in 3OT) and a 21-year playing career with one team (the Gladiators), he announces his retirement on Twitter. The next day, Dr. O'Brien retires after a 30-year teaching career.

Early December 2017, Irish Marvel's jersey No. 44 is raised to the rafters and becomes the first to be retired league-wide.

Couple reunite with the 2009-2010 fifth-grade class in August 2018. Reunion is bittersweet. Group gathers at a funeral chapel to celebrate a young life cut short when Mary Starlett dies from a skydiving accident in the Amazon rainforest. At her homegoing service, each of the 21 ex-classmates (Yingjie, Valerie, Tiny, Superboy, Stevie, Sheet Cake, Shakobe, Rudy, Rebecca, Ray Ray, Ponytail, Lynn, Kathy Rose, Gracie, Fran, Floppy, Dreadhead, Dolf, Charlotte, B-Raid, Betty) wear their class rings on a necklace. What'll happen to Mary Starlett's remains a ring secret.

Boys II Men sings "It's So Hard to Say Goodbye to Yesterday" at the graveside service. At the repast, the old gang takes a picture, swaps contact information, and promises to keep in touch. Out of respect for Mary Starlett nobody asks the burning question on every ex-classmate's mind: Did she or didn't she ever reconsider playing hide the summer sausage?

At home that night, all 21 ex-classmates think about *The Bachelorette* contestant who was virgin-shamed, the stigma around virginity, and imagine what it'd be like to die an adult virgin. Individually, they all concur it's an honorable, yet unfortunate possibility everyone's born with and that S-E-X is highly overrated. They all conclude that not experiencing a well-lived life is far worse than not crossing S-E-X off a bucket list.

Couple's firecracker four is their last possession of the baby ball. In August 2024, the O'Brien children call Ryan Seacrest's radio show. The four squared (4x4) asks Ry Ry to help get Color Me Badd to surprise their parents. In September 2024, quartet sings "All 4 Love" at the couple's 25th silver wedding anniversary party.

None of the couple's senior, junior, or sophomore quads teach or play pro sports. Three out of the freshman final four follow in their father's footsteps. Sofy is the top pro women's basketball draft pick in April 2032. Romy and Tony, rare conjoined twins (one White, one Black) who had separation surgery at six months, are both first-round draft picks for pro men's basketball in June 2032. Cojy is a Pilates instructor and rookie sensation for the Dallas Cowboys in September 2032.

One year later, Irish Marvel is enshrined in the Hall of Fame. Two months thereafter, the basketballer-turned-businessman with a multibillion-dollar empire has his outdoor arena statue unveiled.

By 2040, all the couple's mixed-race offspring have graduated with honors from HBCUs and are happily married. All eight daughters (Viqy, Dixy, Lacy, Katy, Mapy, Nury, Judy, Sofy) have Black husbands. All eight sons (Fily, Zigy, Wavy, Huey, Quby, Romy, Tony, Cojy) have White wives. None of them met their respective spouses at a Black Lives Matter protest, while advocating for the #MeToo movement nor by joining Bumble, Tinder, or Ashley Madison.

Dr. O'Brien auctions her third upgraded wedding ring in 2045 at a fundraiser benefiting the couple's foundation. The winning bidder surprises everyone in a stunning turn of events. Wesley Kimmel formerly known as "The Baby Bachelor" outbids Riley Curry, Apple Martin, Blue Ivy Carter, Suri Cruise, Rocket Williams, "Trick Shot" Titus Ashby, North West, Max Zuckerberg, Jermajesty Jackson, and Prince George.

On September 19, 2049, the senior citizens reach their semicentennial anniversary. After their 50th golden wedding anniversary party, they embark on a 50-day European escapade sponsored by their sweet 16.

Things fell into place later in life for the former Dorothy Bell Okafor. She was a quinquagenarian when society could say that she lived up to the definition of having it all – happy marriage, rewarding career, and great kids.

From that point on, kinfolk and friends believe being a grammy is out of the question for her and predict lotsa grandpets and grandplants. Behind her back, they take wagers for decades that she won't live to see her grandbabies, let alone watch them grow up. Day after the golden girl's 96th birthday, their bleak outlook takes a U-turn in 2051 when she posts a Snapchat photo of her first grandchild.

On February 19, 2067, the remodeled city library where the couple's journey began, is renamed in the O'Brien's honor 68 years later to the date. The renaming is thanks to their generous annual contribution since 1999 and rumored recommendation from Dr. Carla Hayden, the 14th Librarian of Congress. Before the ribbon-cutting ceremony, the out-of-towners tell the story of how they met. He was in town to see a surgeon for a pinky injury. She was in town for a friend's wedding. The two struck up a conversation in the cookbook aisle. During their speech, wellderly couple announce that when their time expires their final resting place will be near a picturesque pond behind the library. Prior to this honor, the seniors hadn't given the subject much thought. Couple only told their kids that they didn't wanna fry in a crematory. They decided burial in Truth or Consequences, New Mexico, would be a nod to their sense of humor and a great reminder for their grandchildren to make good choices during the dash years (read 'The Dash' poem by Linda Ellis).

On September 19, 2074, the islands-in-the-stream couple achieve their 75th diamond wedding anniversary. Three days later, they celebrate the monumental milestone with family (including 31 grandkids, 8 great-grandkids) and friends. The O'Briens open with a bang by doing the iconic dance from the '80s movie *Dirty Dancing* to the hit "(I've Had) The Time of My Life." After that, the gutsy two thank the Almighty for living through the choreography and thank the EMTs on standby backstage. They light candles in memory of those (including all other wedding party) who died during their marriage and talk about being comforted by the resurrection hope. Next, the husband-and-wife team joyfully reminisce about sharing many firsts along their epic journey. After that, husband speaks about doubting Thomases who doubted their partnership would outlast a pro 10-day basketball contract, surviving 18 seasons in a bicoastal long-distance marriage, and gloomy Guses who thought grandparenthood wasn't in the cards for them. Afterward, wife talks about being fortunate her adult years as a single Black female weren't hella messy like BET's Mary Jane and how blessed she feels to vastly surpass the 20-plus year marriage statistic for individuals marrying in their 40s. Lastly, the ex-Tucson, Arizona teacher and ex-Baltimore, Maryland basketeer convey how glad they are never appearing on *Iyanla: Fix My Life*.

When the cool kids get home, they open a letter from Guinness World Records. The notification congratulates them for breaking a record in two different categories: longest married age-gap couple and longest married interracial couple. Immediately, wife fondly remembers her Guinness Book conversation with Dreadhead in 2009 (review page 4, paragraph 2).

On September 22, 2075, (after the medication-free couple made love) spry hubby, 98, asks his supercentenarian spouse during breakfast: "Looking back on your life, are ya disappointed you weren't a hot *young* ma and grandma?" Wifey answers: "Shortly after 40, I stopped grieving what wasn't meant to be and accepted that our Maker had a *different* plan." Hubby finishes his Irish oatmeal and says: "Our Maker making you a hot *old* great-grandma is just as good and pretty darn cool! You're an extraordinary victory story with one of the best come-from-behind wins. What a legacy!" Wifey thinks about the illderly community and recalls the Scripture at Psalms 90:10 speaking about man's lifespan being only 70-80 years even with special mightiness and responds: "I couldn't agree with you more." She washes down a LifeExtension multivitamin with her anti-aging smoothie, gets dressed, and takes a classy selfie standing by 16 blue roses. Unbeknownst to wifey, proud hubby posts a recent bikini pic to her IG with #121YearOldHourglassHottie in honor of National Centenarian's Day. In record-breaking time, she gets the most likes and followers in Instagram's history. Her sensational swimsuit snapshot makes headline news worldwide.

Final/OT →

Locker Room

Hope you enjoyed my 10-year passion project and learned something. I'm asking readers to please assist in publicizing this self-published book through word of mouth, via social media, or by submitting a favorable online review. Your assistance would be much appreciated. If you're not familiar with my two previous self-published releases, check out excerpts at www.LadyCanaday.com.

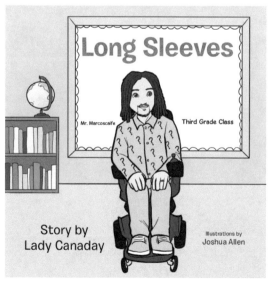

Printed in the United States
By Bookmasters